Endorsements for Never Lose Heart—Sports Heroes Who Overcame the Odds

"We learn timeless lessons from great stories, a truth that Pete Black grasped many years ago. In this inspirational collection of stories, he helps us find within ourselves the resilience essential to finishing well. Highly recommended."

— Andrew Westmoreland, President Emeritus,
Samford University

"In a time when most people are living in fear and doubt, I am encouraged when I read the stories of men and women who refused to give in to their fears knowing they were created to be overcomers. I love this book and strongly recommend Pete Black's *Never Lose Heart – Sports Heroes Who Overcame the Odds*."

— Mike Dubose, Former Head Football Coach,
University of Alabama

"Awesome read! There is a life lesson in every story."

—Steve Savarese, Former Executive Director,
Alabama High School Athletic Association

"As an SEC football official for more than a decade, I've watched plenty of underdogs win when there seemed to be no chance. *Never Lose Heart – Sports Heroes Who Overcame the Odds* is chockful of those kinds of stories, and it will you keep you flipping the pages. It's a great book for those who love to pull for the underdog, and who doesn't."

— James Carter,
Southeastern Conference Football Referee

“I just finished reading Pete Black’s second book *Never Lose Heart: Sports Heroes Who Overcame the Odds*, and I highly recommend it. If you are a pastor, teacher or any kind of public speaker then you know you’re always looking for an interesting and compelling story. In fact, I bet you are like me and perhaps have said, 'I’d give $100 right now for a good story to enhance my message.' You need to look no further for *Sports Heroes Who Overcame the Odds* does just that. You will love this book as I do.”

— Al Baker, Pastor, Evangelist

“I couldn’t put this book down – read it cover-to-cover in one day. Pete has an amazing ability to share stories in a way that make readers want to stand up and cheer as well as self-reflect and become a better person. Every student athlete in Alabama should have a copy of this must-read celebration of sports.”

— Nivada Spurlock, Former Women’s Basketball Coach, Fairfield & Homewood High Schools

“I have known Pete Black for more than four decades. He is a CEO – chief encouragement officer. His book can be used as a daily ‘pep pill’ motivating the reader to be persistent in the pursuit of a goal or dream. I encourage you to get Pete’s book and I know you will find what I did: a reminder of your own life experiences when faced with a decision to continue or quit. *Never Lose Heart – Sports Heroes Who Overcame the Odds* is about dreams, challenges, perseverance and prevailing. One chapter in the book is titled Dream Big – Dare to Fail, which is a common theme in each chapter. Pete is right, ‘It’s always too soon to quit.”

— Johnny Crowe, Florida State University, Sports Hall of Fame

"As a child, one of my favorite books was a collection of sports stories of athletes who overcame long odds or physical injuries or cultural disadvantages to 'rise above.' Having the chance to be a first-hand witness to these types of stories and getting to tell them is a major reason I became a sportswriter. In Never Lose Heart: Sports Heroes Who Overcame the Odds, Pete Black has put together a new compilation of these type of stories. Some will be familiar, some will not, but all demonstrate why sports stories are unique in their power to inspire and encourage us. From Roger Bannister breaking the four-minute mile barrier to Jim Abbott becoming a major league pitcher despite being born with only one hand, Black has compiled stories that remind us that anything is possible. I recommend this book, particularly for younger readers who need to know these stories of people who turned "impossible" situations into inspirational moments and remind us that each of us has the power to change our own lives."

— Ray Melick, Former Sportswriter, *Birmingham News*,
Alabama Sports Writers Hall of Fame

"An inspiring book from an old ball player! I especially enjoyed the baseball stories. My favorite was Nobody Had Ever Seen a Ball Player Like This One. What an awesome story!"

— Brad Bohannon, Head Baseball Coach,
University of Alabama

"Pete is a wonderful guy who has done a fantastic job with this book. The stories provide great messages. The way the book is written allows it to serve as a devotional, if you prefer to read a chapter each day."

— Chris Stewart. Sportscaster,
Crimson Tide Sports Network

NEVER LOSE HEART

SPORTS HEROES WHO OVERCAME THE ODDS

Pete Black

Never Lose Heart—Sports Heroes Who Overcame the Odds
1st edition

BWPublications.com
Florence, Alabama
Library of Congress Control Number: 2021900019
ISBN - 978-1-958273-15-9 Paperback
ISBN - 978-1-958273-14-2 eBook

Published in the United States by Bluewater Publications.
This work is based from the author's personal research and interpretation.
Managing Editor — Angela Broyles
Editor — Rachel Davis
Interior Design — Rachel Davis
Cover Design — Angela Broyles

Jesus told the disciples a story that they might always pray, and never lose heart.
Luke 18:1

Jesus walked the back roads and told stories that changed lives for eternity. Stories can inspire people to chase their dreams, overcome seemingly impossible obstacles, and ignite hope when things seem hopeless.

The road to triumph is full of tests and trials. Every struggle in our life will become a story someday. It will either be a story about how we got stronger and persevered or a story about why we gave up. We can't always choose our struggles, but we can choose which story becomes true.
Dave Willis

TABLE OF CONTENTS

QUITTING MY DREAM: A FOREWORD

It's been forty years since that Friday afternoon in May of 1975. I remember the event just like it was yesterday. I guess forty years from now, should I live that long, that will still be the case? I quit the University of Alabama baseball team and walked off Sewell-Thomas Field for the last time. It was one of the defining moments in my life.

While growing up in the 1950s and 1960s in Monroeville, Alabama what I dreamed about most was being a baseball star. My parents loved sports of any kind and they fueled my dream. I spent countless hours playing ball. I quarterbacked the Monroe County High School football team and was a starting pitcher on the baseball team.

In May of 1971, my dream came true when I signed a baseball scholarship with the University of Alabama. After flirting with the starting pitching rotation as a freshman, I injured my pitching shoulder. Following extensive surgery, the surgeon's prognosis was that I would never be able to pitch again. He advised me to either try another position or give up baseball. Another position? I was a pitcher, and my dream was to pitch for Alabama.

It took a year to rehabilitate my shoulder during a redshirt season. I was stubborn, determined that I was going to make it as a pitcher. During my sophomore and junior seasons, I was relegated to pitching batting practice, never getting in a game. I got so good at throwing batting practice that I was allowed to travel to some away games just to pitch batting practice.

Discouraged but refusing to give up, I continued to work hard. By my senior season, I had learned to throw an excellent changeup. Although the injury had caused me to lose significant velocity on my fastball, I figured if I could master the changeup, the coach might let me pitch. And he did. I pitched in three games as a senior. In all three games, Alabama was either way ahead or way behind. It was embarrassing for me to pitch mop up roles.

As the season progressed, I grew increasingly frustrated with the coach for not allowing me to pitch. After a particularly disappointing loss in Tuscaloosa in early May, my frustration spilled over and I got in an argument with the coach after a game. At the end of our argument, I told him I quit the team. It was a very painful experience.

I called my daddy and told him what happened. He was shocked and no doubt disappointed. He urged me to rethink my decision and to ask the coach if I could return to the team. He told me that if I quit, I would always regret it. I promised him I would think about my decision over the weekend. And I did—all weekend long.

On Monday morning, I scheduled a meeting with the coach for that afternoon. He offered this suggestion, "Finish the season and I'll letter you. You won't have to come back your final year of eligibility." I was stubborn. I quit the team. My dad was right; I have always regretted it.

For more than twenty years after quitting the Alabama baseball team, I had a recurring nightmare. In the dream, I was always trying to make a comeback as a pitcher at Alabama. Sometimes in the dream, I would be pitching in my underwear. In other dreams, I would be in the bullpen warming up, hoping to get in the game, but never getting in. Sometimes, I would get in the game, only to have the game rained out. I always woke up feeling depressed and frustrated.

Over the years I rarely spoke about the experience; it was too painful and embarrassing. Finally, I can talk about it and write about it, but it is still not easy. I quit my dream and it was heart breaking for me. The experience made me hate quitting—in myself, and in others. It made me realize that there is great honor in not quitting. It helped make me more determined. It also caused me to be more encouraging of others to pursue their dreams, and to never give up on them.

Looking back, I can say that the experience caused me to grow and discover things about myself, which otherwise I may never have realized. It changed the course of my life and helped shape who I am. It's also one of the reasons I write these stories, hoping to encourage others not to give up on their dream.

Pete Black

DOING THE IMPOSSIBLE

"Only those who will risk going too far can possibly find out how far one can go."
T.S. Eliot

May 6, 1954 – Oxford University Track – Oxford, England: The day dawned with heavy rain and strong, gusty winds. Because of the weather, he thought about dropping out of the race scheduled for six p.m. that evening. Word had gotten around that he was hoping to break the one-mile world record. By race time, the wind and rain had subsided and 3,000 people lined the track.

Roger Bannister was born in Harrow, England, in 1929. In 1946, as a seventeen-year-old college student at Oxford, he was inspired to begin running by British runner Sydney Wooderson who had set the British record for the mile at 4:04. Bannister's six-foot-two-inch frame and long legs were ideal for the mile run.

By 1952 Bannister was England's top middle-distance runner and a heavy favorite to win the 1,500-meter event in the Helsinki Olympics that year. Although he broke the Olympic record time for the 1,500-meters, so did the three medal winners. Bannister finished a disappointing fourth and failed to medal. He was so upset to have let England down that he considered quitting the sport and focusing on medical school.

After a two-month sabbatical, Bannister set his sights on the impossible—breaking the four-minute mile barrier. The mile record had been stuck at 4:01 for nine years. Several prominent medical journals speculated that it might be physiologically impossible and dangerous for the human body to run that fast.

The featured event, the mile run, began at six p.m. Bannister completed the first lap in second place with a time of 57.5 seconds. At the race mid-way point, he was on a world-record-breaking pace of 1:58. Then his pace slowed, and he completed the third lap at the three-minute mark. In the final lap, with 275 yards to go, Bannister made his move to the front of the pack and outdistanced the field to win the race.

In the era before electronic scoreboards, time was kept with a stopwatch on the track and finish times were announced over a public address system. After a long delay, the voice crackled over the loudspeaker, "Ladies and gentlemen, here is the result of event nine, the one mile. First, R.G. Bannister of Exeter and Merton Colleges in a time which, subject to ratification, is a new track record, British record, European record, and world record—

three minutes and..." The roar of the crowd drowned out the rest of the announcement.

Roger Bannister, a 25-year-old Oxford University medical student, running on his home track, had just done the impossible with a time of 3:59.6 seconds. *Sports Illustrated* dubbed it the most significant athletic event of the twentieth century and featured Bannister on the magazine cover, honoring him as their Sportsman of the Year.

Bannister's sub-four-minute mile record lasted only forty-six days. On June 24, Australian John Landy lowered Bannister's record by almost two seconds when he ran a mile in 3:57.9 in Finland. Within three years, the record was down to 3:54. In the sixty-five years since Roger Bannister did the seemingly impossible, more than 1,300 runners have broken the four-minute mile. The current world record is 3:43 held by Hichan El Guerrouj of Morocco.

A few months after his historic run, Dr. Roger Bannister retired from competitive racing to pursue a career as a neurologist. In July 2012 as part of the summer Olympics in London, 83-year-old running legend Roger Bannister carried the Olympic torch at the site of his historic run, the old track stadium at Oxford that is now named for him. "I almost didn't race that afternoon because of the weather," reminisced Bannister, "I am glad that I did as I might not have gotten another chance."

REFERENCES

"Bannister, 85, Reflects 60 Years After Breaking the Four-Minute Mile." *Sports Illustrated,* May 3, 2014.

Cavendish, Richard. "The First Sub-Four-Minute Mile." History Today, May 5, 2004. https://www.historytoday.com/archive/first-sub-four-minute-mile.

Klein, Christopher. "The First 4-Minute Mile, 60 Years Ago." History.com. A&E Television Networks, May 6, 2014. https://www.history.com/news/the-first-4-minute-mile-60-years-ago.

"Roger Bannister." Wikipedia. Wikimedia Foundation, January 29, 2022. https://en.wikipedia.org/wiki/Roger_Bannister.

CABBIE'S ADVICE SAVES CAREER

"Advice is seldom welcome, and those who need it most like it least."
Samuel Johnson

June 21, 2011 – Petco Park Stadium, San Diego, California: San Diego Padres pitcher Wade LeBlanc listened to the voicemail informing him he was going back to the Padres' Triple-A team in Tucson, Arizona. It was the eighth time in three years he had been sent down to the minor leagues. He knew the drill well: pack up your bags, pick up your airline ticket, and get lost in Tucson. His major league career was at rock bottom. Again.

LeBlanc hailed a cab outside the stadium. "Aren't you Wade LeBlanc?" the driver asked. "Me and my buddies watched you pitch last night." LeBlanc nodded his head, not wanting to be reminded of the previous evening's pitching performance. "You've got good stuff," the cabbie continued. "I don't know. I'm not a player, but maybe you should try raising your arms over your head in your windup." LeBlanc rolled his eyes. That was all the 26-year-old lefty needed on this discouraging day—a San Diego cab driver telling him how to pitch.

LeBlanc was born in Lake Charles, Louisiana, in 1984. He was an outstanding pitcher at Barbe High School and, despite having a fastball that only clocked at 86 mph on his best day, he signed a baseball scholarship with the University of Alabama in 2003. LeBlanc became the first freshman in Alabama history to be chosen by Baseball America as National Freshman of the Year. After a stellar career in Tuscaloosa, he was a second round draft pick of the San Diego Padres.

In 2008, after three seasons in the minor leagues, LeBlanc finally got the call to report to the Padres major league team in August. He pitched in five games with a 1-3 record. During the next three seasons, LeBlanc lived a nomadic existence. He pitched in forty-nine games for the Padres but was frequently sent down to the minors to make room for other pitchers on the roster. He endured all the jokes about his fastball. "LeBlanc throws like he's afraid he will hurt the catcher's hand…He pitches like he's tossing an egg…He pitches like he might break the baseball."

In July 2011 when LeBlanc was sent to Tucson again, he figured his career was over. He told pitching coach Steve Webber he was going to change his windup. What did he have to lose? Instead of keeping his hands close to his chest, he would raise them over his head like the cab driver suggested. In his next start, he pitched seven innings and only gave up one hit.

During LeBlanc's fifteen-year professional career, he has played for seven major league teams, including the Miami Marlins, Houston Astros, New York Yankees, San Diego Mariners, and Baltimore Orioles. He has pitched in 240 games with a record of 45 wins and 47 losses. In 2018, his best season, he pitched in 32 games and went 9-5 for Seattle.

In March 2021, at age thirty-six and despite being the oldest man on the Baltimore Orioles team, the veteran pitcher reported to spring training looking for a key role on the pitching staff. LeBlanc still holds his hands over his head in his windup. There have been plenty of potholes and perhaps not enough pinnacles in Wade LeBlanc's career, but he's still pitching. He says, "I think I could have been more successful earlier in my career if it wasn't for the self-doubt and stubbornness. If you had asked me when I was with the Padres at age 26 years if I would still be pitching a decade later, I would have told you no."

Wade LeBlanc credits the cab driver's advice with helping to save his career. Although a small change, moving his hands above his head in his pitching delivery made him a better pitcher. He learned to accept the advice of others and not to be so stubborn. And along the way, he learned how to survive through all the ups and downs in his career.

REFERENCES

Brock, Corey. "How advice from a cab driver helped save Wade's LeBlanc's career." *The Athletic*, April 27, 2018.

Grierson, Bruce. "Why It's So Hard to Take Advice." *Reader's Digest,* December 2019.

University of Alabama Athletics. "Wade Leblanc Named Baseball America's National Freshman of the Year." University of Alabama Athletics. University of Alabama Athletics, May 10, 2016. https://rolltide.com/news/2004/6/25/Wade_LeBlanc_Named_Baseball_America_s_National_Freshman_of_the_the_Year.aspx.

"Wade Leblanc Stats." Baseball Reference. Accessed April 1, 2022. https://www.baseball-reference.com/players/l/leblawa01.shtml.

"Wade Leblanc Stats, Fantasy & News." MLB.com. Accessed April 1, 2022. https://www.milb.com/player/wade-leblanc-453281.

A GAMBLE AT BEST

"A bend in the road is not the end of the road...unless we fail to make the turn."
Helen Keller

November 1996 – Ann Arbor, Michigan: Tom called his mother in California ready to quit the University of Michigan football team. He had been seventh on the quarterback depth chart as a freshman and received a red shirt. Now, his sophomore season had been a big disappointment. A pre-season appendix operation took thirty pounds off his already skinny frame. He only threw five passes during the season—the first one of which had been intercepted and returned for a touchdown. But Tom's mother encouraged him to stick it out. "The road to your destiny is never straight. There will be lots of twists and turns. You know that. Talk to your coach." Tom sought out the athletic department counselor who persuaded him not to quit or transfer back to a California school closer to home.

Tom Brady was born in San Mateo, California in 1977. Though he was not the fastest or most talented high school football player, he was a coach's dream. After school in the off-season, he went home, did his homework, and then headed to the gym for a three-hour workout. His coach was so impressed with Brady's work ethic that he adopted his rigorous workout regimen for the entire team.

Brady's four-year career stats at Junipero Serra High School—thirteen touchdown passes, a fifty-three percent pass completion rate, and a total of 3,700 yards passing—did not land him on the college recruiting radar. At 6'4" and a 175 pounds, he was considered too skinny and too slow for big-time college football. The only Division I school to offer a scholarship was Michigan.

Brady experienced more disappointment during his third season as quarterback for the Wolverines. He played in only four games, completing twelve of fifteen passes for 100 yards. During his junior year, Brady split playing time with another quarterback and, once again, thought about quitting the team. His big break did not come until the eighth game of his senior year when Brady finally became the starting quarterback. He led the team to three straight wins and a 35-34 victory over the University of Alabama in the 1999 Orange Bowl.

The NFL scouting report on Brady read: "A skinny beanpole, does not run well, better arm than people give credit for, smart, and hardworking—a gamble at best." But Coach

Bill Belichick of the New England Patriots saw something in Brady and took the gamble. The Patriots drafted Tom Brady 199th, in the sixth and final round of the 2000 draft.

In 2001, Drew Bledsoe, the Patriots starting quarterback, was injured in the second game, and Brady got his chance. In a Cinderella season, the 23-year-old became the youngest quarterback ever to win a Super Bowl. The Patriots traded Bledsoe after that season.

Today, 44-year-old Brady is still an NFL quarterback, having been traded to the Tampa Bay Bucs in 2020 where he won his unprecedented seventh Super Bowl. He holds the distinction of being the youngest and oldest quarterback to win a Super Bowl, and he is the only player to have been the Super Bowl Most Valuable Player five times. Selected to 14 Pro-Bowls, Brady is also the winningest quarterback in NFL history.

The slow, skinny, gamble-at-best Brady never quit. He thought about it many times while at Michigan, but he followed his mother's advice and stuck it out. NFL analysts consider Tom Brady the biggest steal in the history of the NFL draft. The chances of a sixth-round draft pick winning a Super Bowl are five percent.

REFERENCES

Gaines, Cork. "How the Patriots Drafted a Hall of Fame Quarterback in the 6th Round." *Business Insider Magazine,* May 8, 2014.

Geoffreys, Clayton. *Tom Brady: The Inspiring Story of one of Football's Greatest Quarterbacks.* Create Space Publishing, June 28, 2015.

"Tom Brady Biography." Encyclopedia of World Biography. Accessed March 24, 2022. https://www.notablebiographies.com/news/A-Ca/Brady-Tom.html.

"Tom Brady – Quarterback for the New England Patriots." www.nfl.com.

LONG-LEGGED LADY

"Nothing feels better than doing what other people say you can't do."
Kylie Francis

May 7, 1988 – Kentucky Derby – Louisville, Kentucky: The women came early. They came in record numbers with their painted signs and their flamboyant, frilly hats. Believing the bigger the hat, the better the luck, they filed into Churchill Downs—the most famous horse track in America—and they placed their bets, hoping it was going to be a day for the one filly in the field of sixteen colts.

They came to cheer for Winning Colors, a tall, leggy, athletic gray horse with white splotches across her face. At 1,100 pounds, she was the biggest horse in the race. Only two fillies, Regret (1915) and Genuine Risk (1980) had ever won the Kentucky Derby in its 115-year history. The odds were against Winning Colors.

Horse racing fans mostly staked their money on Forty Niner, the champion two-year-old colt, or undefeated

Private Terms. Few people thought about placing their paycheck on Winning Colors, who had only been raced five times.

Eugene Klein was the owner of Winning Colors. He had sold his San Diego Chargers NFL team to focus on his new passion: thoroughbred racing. Winning Colors was trained by Wayne Lukas, the nation's most successful trainer. In the past decade, Lukas had won every major race. Only one goal eluded him; he had entered twelve horses in the Derby without a win, and Lukas and Klein were anxious "to get the Derby monkey off their back."

Lukas had grown up training quarter horses in Texas and Oklahoma. He knew from experience that thoroughbred fillies could run against the males and beat them in prestigious races. However, Lukas's last filly in the 1984 Derby finished dead last. So, when Winning Colors made the seventeen-horse field, the laughing and joking by other owners and trainers began.

Was Winning Colors the filly to break the curse and win the Run for the Roses? Lukas and those who knew her best were convinced. After she won her second race in December 1987, Winning Colors' stable hands pooled their meager savings. They drove from Santa Anita, California, (the horse's home track) to Las Vegas to bet $2,000 on Winning Colors to win the Kentucky Derby at 100-1 odds.

Winning Colors lost in her first California race in February 1988. There was nothing to indicate she could compete with the boys in Louisville. But a month later, when she blew away eight colts by seven lengths, Lukas decided to give her a shot in one of the best fields in the Derby history.

The first Saturday in May was a beautiful cloudless day. At 6:03 p.m., when the bell sounded, as was her custom, Winning Colors took control of the lead from the start. She opened up a four-length lead in the backstretch and maintained it through the turn. With just over six football fields remaining, a win in the Derby seemed imminent, but Winning Colors had never run a mile and a quarter before. Lukas feared she might tire and fall back. Forty Niner and Private Terms were quickly closing while the long-legged gray filly was obviously tiring.

Jockey Gary Stevens left his whip idle. Instead, he let the reins out a notch. Winning Colors got the message. Time to let it all out and head for home. Stevens felt the surge as the big horse found another gear. Winning Colors dug deep in the final 12 seconds to win by a neck over Private Terms.

The women in attendance rocked Churchill Downs, and Winning Colors' Kentucky Derby win erased a decade of heartbreak for Eugene Klein and Wayne Lukas. She was the clear choice for the champion three-year old filly in 1988 and her legacy as a Kentucky Derby winner will live forever.

In 2000, Winning Colors was inducted into the National Horse Racing Hall of Fame. She lived until 2008 when, at the ripe old age of twenty-three, she died at her post-racing home at Green Tree Farms in Lexington, Kentucky. In 2015, Sports Illustrated named Winning Colors one of the 10 Most Memorable Horses in Kentucky Derby History, and she remains one of three fillies to ever win the Kentucky Derby.

REFERENCES

Angst, Frank. "Sucher – Breeder of Two Hall of Famers, Dies." *Blood Horse Magazine*, February, 2015.

Mark, Paul. *The Greatest Gambling Story Ever Told: A True Tale of Three Gamblers, The Kentucky Derby, and the Mexican Cartel.* Authority Publishing, 2020.

Mieszersk, Bob. "1988 Derby Winner Winning Colors Dies." Los Angeles Times, February 19, 2008.

Nack, William. "Lady's Day." *Sports Illustrated Vault*, May 16,1988. https://vault.si.com/vault/1969/07/14/43010.

"Winning Colors Euthanized." *Blood Horse Magazine,* February19, 2008.999

"Winning Colors." *National Museum of Racing & Hall of Fame.* www.racingmuseum.org

THE LEGEND OF NO. 42

"Jackie, there's virtually nobody on our side. No owner, no umpires, very few newspapermen. And I'm afraid that many fans may be hostile. We'll be in a tough position. We can win only if we can convince the world that I am doing this because you're a great ballplayer and a fine gentleman."
Branch Rickey

1945 – Brooklyn, New York: Branch Rickey, the owner of the Brooklyn Dodgers, was deeply concerned that there were no Black players in Major League Baseball. He knew baseball needed to change, but he knew it would be challenging to break the color barrier. He was willing to take the risk, but his main challenge was to find the right Black player. He needed a man who was not only a great baseball player, but also someone with tremendous courage and impeccable character. He found his man playing for the Kansas City Monarchs.

In 1919, Jack Roosevelt "Jackie" Robinson was born in Georgia to sharecroppers. When he was six months old, his father left home, leaving his mother to raise five children. She moved the family to Pasadena, California, to be near relatives. While she found a job as a maid, Jackie found the ball fields. After high school, he became the first athlete at UCLA to win varsity letters in four sports: baseball, football, basketball, and track. In 1941, Jackie was named to the All-American football team as a running back.

After UCLA and a two-year stint in the Army, Jackie signed to play with the Kansas City Monarchs in the Negro Baseball League. After his first season, he was shocked to get a call from Branch Rickey offering him a contract to play for the Dodgers. The deal included a big salary increase and a "turn the other cheek" clause. Jackie agreed to maintain his dignity and cool regardless of the racial insults that he might experience.

After playing one year in the minor league, on April 15, 1947, the opening day of the season, Jackie Robinson made his major league debut at first base for the Brooklyn Dodgers. He took the field to a chorus of boos from the hometown crowd.

The level of racial prejudice that surfaced during the season was worse than Rickey anticipated. Baseball fans everywhere yelled racial obscenities at Jackie and often threw things at him. Several of Jackie's teammates quit the team instead of continuing to play with him. In ballparks around the league, players refused to play when the Dodgers came to town. Opposing pitchers frequently threw pitches at Jackie's head. In most towns, he had to stay in different hotels and eat in separate restaurants from his teammates. But, despite the jeers, catcalls, and death threats against him and his family, Jackie honored his agreement with Rickey by not reacting to the fans.

Off the field, the season was a nightmare for Jackie and his wife, Rachel. He thought about quitting after most of the 154 games. Jackie had entered a world where being a good baseball player wasn't going to be enough. An entire nation was watching him, and the majority was pulling against him. He bore the heavy burden of great expectations, but realizing the stage was bigger than he was, Jackie hung in there through the difficult season.

The stress that Jackie carried wasn't apparent when he was on the field. He had an outstanding first season, and his twelve home runs helped the Dodgers win the National League pennant for only the third time in history. Jackie stole a league-leading twenty-nine bases and was voted National League Rookie of the Year.

Over the next two years Jackie's performance and exemplary character won over baseball fans, and he opened the door for other Black players. In 1949, he led the league in batting average and stolen bases on his way to winning the National League Most Valuable Player award. In 1955, Jackie helped lead the Brooklyn Dodgers to their first World Series win over their crosstown rival the New York Yankees.

Jackie Robinson retired in 1956, and in 1962, he was elected to the Baseball Hall of Fame. In 1997, to celebrate the 50th anniversary of his integrating baseball, every major league team permanently retired his number 42. He is the only major league player to have ever received this honor.

REFERENCES

Helgeland, Brian, dir. *42: The True Story of an American Legend*, 2013; Burbank, CA: Warner Brothers Pictures.

Henry, Ed and King, Larry. *42 Faith: The Rest of the Jackie Robinson Story.* Nelson Publishing, April 4, 2017.

History.com Editors. "Jackie Robinson." History.com. A&E Television Networks, October 29, 2009. https://www.history.com/topics/black-history/jackie-robinson.

"Jackie Robinson." Biography.com. A&E Networks Television, October 15, 2021. https://www.biography.com/athlete/jackie-robinson.

WORLD'S GREATEST ATHLETE

"You have a choice. You can throw in the towel, or you can use it to wipe the sweat off your face."
Les Brown

October 19, 1968 – Mexico City, Mexico: A light rain began to fall in the late afternoon making the mid-50s temperature seem even colder. The lights were on at Olympic Stadium as the athletes prepared for the high jump, the final event in the two-day decathlon competition. Heading into the high jump, Bill Toomey—America's hope for the gold medal—held a slight lead over two German competitors.

As Toomey shivered in the rain waiting for the high jump to start, he remembered back four years earlier to the 1964 Olympics in Tokyo. Disappointed that he narrowly missed making the U.S. team, he paid his own way to Tokyo. After having won six consecutive Olympic gold medals, Toomey watched from the stands as America finished fourth in the decathlon.

Born in Philadelphia in 1939, Bill Toomey was twelve years old when he severely cut the muscles and nerves in this right hand while playing with a piece of ceramic pottery. Five surgeries were necessary to repair the nerve damage, but Toomey's right hand would always be partially paralyzed.

Despite the injury, Toomey went out for the track team at Worcester High School in Worcester, Massachusetts. He never told the coach about his hand out of concern it might be regarded as an excuse. For almost two years, Toomey tried to use his left hand in track events, but finally gave up and competed successfully right-handed.

Toomey attended the University of Colorado where he was an all-around track and field athlete. He competed in the pentathlon, long jump, javelin throw, 200-meter run, discus throw, and 1,500-meter run. By his own admission, he was not outstanding in any single event. While at Colorado, Toomey won four American Amateur Association National titles in the pentathlon.

Toomey returned from Tokyo determined to win the decathlon and bring the gold medal back to the U.S. in 1968. However, the odds of the 29-year-old decathlete winning a gold medal were slim. No one had ever won the decathlon at age twenty-nine. Despite the odds, Toomey developed a detailed four-year training plan. He focused on improving his running, hurdles, and high jump techniques.

Toomey experienced one setback after another. In 1966, he spent four months in the hospital with hepatitis. Radiation treatments for the liver ailment almost ended his career. After recovering from hepatitis, Toomey got mononucleosis which sidelined him for two more months. A year later, he was in a car accident that fractured his kneecap. The injury required three months of rehab and valuable time out of his training schedule.

Despite his lack of preparation, Toomey made the U.S. team and arrived in Mexico City in October 1968. On the first day of the decathlon, he set a new world record of 45.68 seconds in the 400-meter run, his best event. However, he had pulled a leg muscle at the tape, and it hampered him throughout the second day's events. Now he faced the high jump, his worst event.

With the rain lightly falling, Toomey's goal medal was just a successful high jump away. He stood quietly visualizing himself clearing the bar. To win the gold, he would need more than physical talent. He would need to draw on the emotion created by years of adversity.

Toomey missed on his first two attempts to clear the bar. Knowing what was at stake, the stadium was pin-drop quiet as Toomey contemplated his final attempt. The eruption of 72,000 people could be heard for several miles as Bill Toomey easily sailed over the 6-foot-6-inch bar—a new personal best—to reclaim the gold medal for the U.S. and earn the distinction of "World's Greatest Athlete."

Bill Toomey will always be remembered as one of the greatest decathletes in Olympic history. At 6-foot-1-inch and 190 pounds, he was often smaller than many of the athletes, but his heart was bigger than most. Toomey's success can be attributed less to talent and more to an unwillingness to quit when the cards were stacked against him.

REFERENCES

"Bill Toomey." *Team USA*. Accessed March 27, 2022. https://www.teamusa.org/Hall-of-Fame/Hall-of-Fame-Members/Bill-Toomey.

"Bill Toomey, Track and Field." U.S. Olympic and Paralympic Museum. www.usopm.org

"Bill Toomey, 1971 Inductee." Colorado Sports Hall of Fame. www.coloradosports.org

Reed, William. "The Ineligible Married Man – Bill Toomey says it's kind of tragic being the best decathlete in the world and (SOB!) not being allowed to compete." *Sports Illustrated Vault*, April 12, 1971. www.si.com.

JIMMY V

"Don't give up...don't ever give up."
Jim Valvano

March 4, 1993 – Annual ESPY Awards, Madison Square Garden, NYC: "And the winner of this year's Arthur Ashe Courage Award is…" the announcer paused. "… Jim Valvano, ESPN broadcaster and former head basketball coach at North Carolina State University." Assisted by his good friend and fellow ESPN broadcaster Dick Vitale, and accompanied by loud cheering, Valvano slowly walked to the stage.

"First of all, I'll never forget this night," Valvano told those gathered. "I am honored to be mentioned in the same breath as Arthur Ashe. As you know, I am fighting cancer, and I don't know how long I have left. Time is very precious to me, so I'm going to speak longer than the other award recipients. I have some things I would like to say…"

Jimmy Valvano grew up in a large Italian family in Queens, New York. An outstanding basketball player in high school, he received a scholarship to play point guard at Rutgers University. As a senior, he led the team to a third-place finish in the National Invitation Tournament. After graduation, Valvano began his coaching career as an assistant at Rutgers.

Valvano's 25-year coaching career included stops at Johns Hopkins, Connecticut, and Iona, before coaching from 1980 to 1990 at North Carolina State. His 1983 Cinderella team beat the heavily favored Houston Cougars to win the NCAA national championship.

In 1990, after his hall of fame coaching career, Valvano retired and joined ESPN as a broadcaster. Two years later, while playing golf in Spain, he noticed a pain in his groin. He assumed it was related to his golf game. However, two months later Valvano was diagnosed with metastatic adrenal adenocarcinoma. What Valvano had initially attributed to back pain turned out to be an advanced and aggressive form of cancer. With chemo, doctors gave him a year to live, at best.

Sixteen months later, during Valvano's acceptance speech at the ESPYs, he continued, "I urge all of you to enjoy your life…the precious moments that you have. Every minute that I have left, I will thank God. And in the days that I have left, I will work as hard as I can for research to defeat this dreaded disease. It may not save my life, but it may save the lives of my three little daughters."

Valvano concluded, "One in four will have cancer in their lifetime. And yet, we take cancer for granted. We need more money for cancer research. I am excited to announce tonight that, with the support of ESPN, we will be starting the Jimmy V Foundation for Cancer Research. Our motto is 'Don't give up…don't ever give up.'"

Jim Valvano died just 60 days later, April 29 at age 47. His legacy is not the 1983 national championship or being selected to the basketball hall of fame or winning the Arthur Ashe Courage Award—although those are important achievements. Valvano's legacy, the Jimmy V foundation, continues to be at the forefront of the war on cancer more than four decades later.

For the past twenty-eight years, the foundation has funded cancer research programs for scientists who focus on innovative cures for cancer. So far, more than $260 million has been raised and the V Foundation is saving lives every day.

Valvano never gave in to his cancer. He refused to take narcotics for the pain; twenty-four Advil tablets were usually enough to get him through the day at ESPN. Invariably when he left chemo, sick and bent from the pain, fans asked how he was doing. "Hanging in there… hanging in there," he would smile while signing autographs. Cancer took away Valvano's physical abilities, but it couldn't rob him of his heart and soul.

Duke University Head Basketball Coach Mike Krzyzewski was a close friend of Valvano and was with him during his last days. Krzyzewski will never forget Valvano's words to him during this time, "I know I'm going die. I won't beat cancer, but I'm going to win. I'll be there in the end when we finally beat cancer."

REFERENCES

"ESPY Awards Speech." V Foundation, December 22, 2021. https://www.v.org/about/remembering-jim/espy-awards-speech/.

"Jim Valvano." Wikipedia. Wikimedia Foundation, February 22, 2022. https://en.wikipedia.org/wiki/Jim_Valvano.

Keegan, Kayla. "The Untold Story of Jimmy V's Iconic ESPY Awards Speech." *Good Housekeeping Magazine*, July 11, 2019.

Smith, Gary. "As Time Runs Out – Gravely Ill with Cancer, Jim Valvano if Fighting for His Life the Same Way He Coached Basketball, by Learning All He Can, Talking up a Storm and Insisting on the Last Shot." *Sports Illustrated,* January 11, 1993.

BABE'S MISSING BAT

"I've seen them. Men, women, kids who were hoping to get his name on a torn, dirty piece of paper, or hoping for a grunt of recognition, when they said, 'Hi Babe.' He never let them down. Not once. He was the greatest crowd-pleaser of them all."
Waite Hoyt

December 2, 2004 – Sotheby Auction, New York City: More than 300 people filled the large auction hall at Sotheby's Auction House. They had come for a huge sports memorabilia auction. Babe Ruth's home run bat, which christened a brand-new Yankee stadium in 1923, was the auction's centerpiece.

The excitement in the room was palpable, and as the bidding began for her old bat, Marcia Tejada sat a few rows back from the auctioneer and watched the action in amazement. It started fast at $400,000 and, within a minute, the bat sold for $1.26 million—the most money ever paid for a baseball bat. An anonymous East Coast investor purchased it.

Babe Ruth was born in 1895 in Pigtown, a poor waterfront neighborhood in Baltimore, Maryland. His father ran a saloon, and the family lived in a small apartment upstairs. Neither Ruth's busy father nor his sickly mother had much time for the mischievous youngster who skipped school, roamed the streets, and stole from merchants.

At age eight, after several incidents with the police, Ruth landed in St. Mary's Industrial School for Boys, a Catholic reformatory and orphanage. He spent twelve years there. Father Mathias, one of the teachers, first introduced Ruth to baseball as a young teen. A big-league scout discovered eighteen-year-old Ruth playing baseball at the orphanage and signed him to a contract.

Ruth pitched for the Boston Red Sox from 1914 to 1919. Although he was an outstanding pitcher, he was an even better hitter. After being traded to the New York Yankees in 1919, Ruth became the best home run hitter in baseball.

Before the first game ever played in Yankee Stadium, April 18, 1923, Ruth told reporters, "I'd give a year of my life if I could hit a home run in this new ballpark." It happened in the third inning against Boston. Ruth's towering home run, a three-run shot, christened the new stadium which was later dubbed "The House That Ruth Built." The home run was the climax of a spectacular grand opening and set the stage for the Yankees first of twenty-seven World Series championships

A few weeks later, Ruth, who always had a heart for children's causes and young ballplayers, donated the bat to the *Los Angeles Evening Herald*. He signed it, "To the Boy Home Run King of Los Angeles, Babe Ruth, May 7, 1923." The bat was awarded to young Victor Orsatti, a high school senior, who led the city in home runs.

Orsatti treasured the bat for more than sixty years. Before his death in 1984, he willed the bat, along with some of his personal items, to Marcia Tejada, his home healthcare nurse. Clueless to its value, Tejada stuck the bat under her bed where it remained for twenty years. In 2004, she discovered the bat and took it to a sports memorabilia store in Los Angeles. The shocked owner suggested that Tejada auction off the long-time missing bat and put her in touch with Sotheby's.

Tejada used several hundred thousand dollars from the auction proceeds to start a restaurant, a life-long dream. However, she donated most of the money to a children's charity to honor the Home Run king.

Babe Ruth was the first player to hit 60 home runs in a season, and his career record of 714 home runs stood for 34 years until Henry Aaron broke it in 1974. Ruth signed hundreds of baseballs for kids during his career, but he signed less than a dozen bats. More than 80 years after his dramatic opening day home run, his missing bat, a 36-inch, 46-ounce Louisville slugger, fetched more than half of what Yankee Stadium cost to build in 1923.

The Babe loved kids and they loved him. He was always happy to sign autographs, take pictures with children, and visit them in hospitals. According to Tejada, "The bat was only valuable because Babe Ruth's name was on it. The only reasonable thing to do was something that would honor his life."

REFERENCES

"Babe Ruth's Bat Sold by Sotheby's." CNNMoney. Cable News Network. December 2, 2004

"Babe Ruth." Encyclopedia Britannica. Encyclopedia Britannica, inc. Accessed March 30, 2022. https://www.britannica.com/biography/Babe-Ruth.

"Babe Ruth Stats." Baseball. Accessed March 30, 2022. https://www.baseball-reference.com/players/r/ruthba01.shtml.

Getlin, Josh. "With One Swing (of the gavel), Ruth's Bat Hits $1.26 Million." *New York Times,* December 3, 2004.

"Introduction." Babe Ruth | Official Site. Accessed March 30, 2022. http://www.baberuth.com/.

Rovell, Darren. "The Bambino Strikes Again." ESPN, December 2, 2004.

"SportsCards Plus & Sotheby's to Sell Babe Ruth's Storied Bat." PSA, August 9, 2004. https://www.psacard.com/Articles/ArticleView/4222/sportscards-plus-sothebys-sell-babe-ruths-storied-bat.

ON TOP OF THE WORLD

"What's in you is stronger than what's in your way."
Erik Weihenmayer

August 6, 1996 – El Capitan – Yosemite National Park, California: For three days, Ed Weihenmayer had been following his 28-year-old son Erik's climb up the 3,000-foot granite wall called El Capitan. Ed sat in a lawn chair with his telescope, craning his neck as Erik and his three buddies slowly climbed higher and higher. A few feet away from Ed, Erik's wife, Ellie, could not bear to look as the climbers approached 2,500 feet.

When a crowd of tourists walked up, Ed pointed and proudly said, "That's my son way up there." A large woman in a floppy hat asked, "Aren't you afraid?" Ed responded, "Sure, especially since he's blind." "Blind?" she repeated in astonishment. "And you let him do that? You are his father!" She turned to her husband, "Let's go honey, I think we've seen enough." As she headed for the car,

Ed couldn't resist, "And he also skydives."

Born in Princeton, New Jersey, Erik Weihenmayer was diagnosed with retinoschisis, a rare eye disease, at fifteen months old. Ed and Ellen Weihenmayer were determined to create opportunities for their son to do the things that other boys could do despite his blindness. When Erik was six, Ed took the training wheels off his bicycle and taught him to ride. When Erik crashed, which was often, Ed would always pick him up.

Erik excelled at wrestling in high school and made it to the National Junior Freestyle Championship in Iowa. At age sixteen, he discovered rock climbing at a summer camp and fell in love with the sport. He was a natural. Aided by his blindness, Erik was especially adept in feeling the little knobs, cracks, and fissures in the rock. To him, it was like solving a puzzle in the rock.

Erik graduated from Boston College with a degree in English and moved to Phoenix to become a teacher and wrestling coach. In his early 20s, he married Ellie. With her support, his love of rock climbing eventually expanded to mountain climbing. Never one to back down from a challenge, Erik climbed increasingly difficult peaks.

In 1995, Erik's friends thought he was a fool when a climbing buddy challenged him to climb 20,300-foot Denali in Alaska, the highest peak in North America. With the help of several other climbers, he did it. A year later, Erik was scaling El Capitan as his father nervously watched from below.

On May 25, 2001, supported by a $250,000 sponsorship from the National Blind Federation and a 19-member team, Erik became the first blind person to stand on top of the world when he reached the summit of Mt. Everest, the world's tallest mountain at more than 29,000 feet. *Time* magazine honored Erik by featuring him on the cover.

Only ten percent of the climbers who attempt Mt. Everest make it to the top. Under the best conditions it is physically, mentally, and emotionally grueling for elite climbers. Climbing experts say the idea of a blind climber even attempting this dangerous feat is beyond ridiculous—it is absurd.

According to *Time,* "What Erik Weihenmayer achieved is hard for a sighted person to comprehend. There is no way to put what Erik has done into perspective because no one has ever done anything like it. It is a unique achievement. One that, in the truest sense, pushes the limits of what man is capable of."

Erik has also completed the Seven Summits Challenge by climbing the highest mountain on each of the seven continents. He is the only blind climber and one of only 500 climbers who has climbed into this exclusive club. His Mt. Everest climb ranks number four on the list of the greatest ascents of the tallest mountain on earth.

Today, Erik continues to climb and manages "No Barriers," a nonprofit organization he founded. The organization teaches outdoor skills to physically challenged people. He is also one of the world's most sought-after motivational speakers.

REFERENCES

"About Erik." Erik Weihenmayer. Accessed March 30, 2022. https://erikweihenmayer.com/about-erik/.

"Erik Weihenmayer and Touch the Top, Inc.." No Barriers, January 10, 2019. https://nobarriersusa.org/about/partners/erik-weihenmayer-touch-the-top/.

Glusac, Elaine. "Conquering Mt. Everest, Against All Odds." New York Times, October 19, 2018.

Weihenmayer, Erik. *Touch the Top of the World.* New York: Penguin Group Publishing, February 2001.

Weihenmayer, Erik. "A Blind Ascent: Summiting Everest Without Sight." Outside Magazine, May 14, 2012.

MAMA'S GRIT

"Listen, I come from the most screwed up dysfunctional situation. Violence, police at your house, your dad's gone and nowhere to live. I want people to know, if I can make it, anybody can make it."
Dabo Swinney

1975 – Pelham, Alabama: Young Dabo witnessed things no child should see. Ervil Swinney, his alcoholic father, didn't always come home at night, and on the nights he did, he often fought with his wife, Carol. Several times the police were called to their home. When Dabo was in the seventh grade, Ervil lost the family appliance repair business and their house on Ashcroft Road.

Ervil and Carol divorced when Dabo was a junior in high school. Carol rented an apartment but couldn't pay the rent, and they were evicted three months later. During his senior year, Dabo and Carol were homeless. They moved in with the family of a high school classmate. Dabo slept on the living room floor while Carol shared a bed with the friend's mom. Despite his troubled home life, Dabo was an honor student and a three-sport athlete at Pelham High School.

Dabo got his love of Alabama football from Ervil and got his grit and tenacity from Carol. At two years old, Carol had been stricken with polio and spent eleven years in the Birmingham Crippled Children's Hospital. She wore a body cast to correct severe scoliosis and did not learn to walk until age thirteen.

With the help of federal student aid and loans, Dabo attended the University of Alabama. At 6 feet tall and 165 pounds, it took some convincing of the coaching staff, but Dabo fulfilled a dream in 1989 by walking on as a wide receiver on the Crimson Tide's football team. Of the forty-five walk-on players, Dabo was one of only two who received a scholarship.

When Dabo moved to Tuscaloosa, Carol couldn't afford housing for him plus her apartment in Birmingham, so Dabo invited her to live with him and his roommate at their Fountaine Bleau apartment. Her fried chicken, chili, and chocolate chip cookies were teammate favorites. Each morning, Carol woke at 5 a.m. and drove 50 miles to her $8 an hour job at a Birmingham department store. In addition to his college classes and football responsibilities, Dabo worked weekends cleaning gutters and doing odd jobs.

Dabo and Carol roomed together in Tuscaloosa for three years. Dabo made the starting rotation at wide receiver and played on three Alabama football teams, including Coach Gene Stallings'1992 National Championship team, which beat Miami 34-13 in the Sugar Bowl. Dabo made the All-SEC Academic team twice and earned a bachelor's degree in business administration.

After graduating, Dabo served as a graduate assistant on the Alabama coaching staff while earning a master's in business administration. In 1995, while Dabo was interviewing for jobs in the business world, Coach Stallings surprised him with an offer to coach receivers. Dabo remained on the staff until 2001 when Coach Mike Dubose and the entire staff were fired.

After getting fired, Dabo took a two-year hiatus from coaching and sold real estate in Birmingham. In 2003, Clemson University football coach, Tommy Bowden, offered him a job to coach receivers at Clemson. Realizing that his heart was in coaching, Dabo took a pay cut and accepted the job. Bowden later promoted him to recruiting coordinator.

During a difficult 2008 season, Tommy Bowden resigned after six games. To the surprise of the football world, Dabo was promoted to interim head coach. He turned the season around, took the team to a bowl game, and was named the team's permanent head coach in December of that year.

In fall of 2021, Dabo Swinney will begin his fourteenth season at the helm for the Clemson Tigers. His teams have won seven conference championships, made six straight college football playoff appearances, won two

National Championships, and he has been honored with a National Coach of the Year award.

Today, Dabo refers to Carol as "the mama of the millennium." She has remarried, lives in Birmingham, and never misses a Clemson game. Carol has her own bedroom at Dabo's house in Clemson. Her favorite quote from her favorite coach is: "Sometimes when life isn't perfect, it's BYOG time. You gotta 'bring your own guts.'" She and Dabo know a little about that.

REFERENCES

Brady, Erik and Berkowitz, Steve. "College Football Coaches Continue to See Salary Explosion." *USA Today,* November 20, 2012.

Bonesteel, Matt. "Here's Why Dabo Swinney Brought His Mom with Him to College." *Washington Post,* January 6, 2016.

"Dabo Swinney." Clemson Tigers Official Athletics Site. https://clemsontigers.com/, February 11, 2022. https://clemsontigers.com/coaches/dabo/.

"Dabo Swinney Travels Long Road to Restore Clemson to Prominence." Yahoo! Sports. Yahoo!, September 19, 2012. https://sports.yahoo.com/news/ncaaf--dabo-swinney-travels-long-road-to-restore-clemson-to-prominence.html.

"Dabo Swinney." Wikipedia. Wikimedia Foundation, March 23, 2022. https://en.wikipedia.org/wiki/Dabo_Swinney.

Williams, Larry. "Against All Odds." www.clemsonrivals.com, November 26, 2008.

MRS. MORHARD

"The question is not who is going to let me; it's who is going to stop me."
Ayn Rand

Sunday, September 28, 1941 – League Park - Cleveland, Ohio: Josephine Morhard took her seat behind the first base dugout in the venerable old ballpark. Home of the Cleveland Indians, it was the place where Babe Ruth hit his 500th home run.

On this cool afternoon, it would host the country's first Little World Series championship between the Little Cleveland Indians and Little St. Louis Cardinals. The game would be the crowning moment for the first boy's baseball league that Morhard had pioneered four years earlier. It had not been easy. But nothing in her life had ever been.

Morhard was the eleventh of seventeen children born to a French immigrant farmer in Bessemer, Pennsylvania. At twelve, tired of her father's beatings, she ran away from home and found work as a maid. In 1915, after bouncing from one low-paying job to another, she moved to Cleveland and started her own stenography business at age twenty-four.

Twice Morhard married alcoholics who became mean and physically abusive when they drank. Her first marriage lasted seven years. The second lasted nine years and ended a few months before the 1929 stock market crash. At age thirty-nine, she was pregnant with a son, Albert, and the owner of a struggling butcher shop one mile from League Park.

By age eight, Albert was getting in trouble at school. Morhard feared he would grow up to be like his father. Working six days a week at the butcher shop left her little time for proper supervision. When Albert played baseball, he stayed out of trouble; but the neighborhood houses had no yards, so the boys played baseball in the streets with their nailed-up bats and old balls while cars whizzed past.

In the spring of 1937, Morhard had an idea: She would create a boys baseball team for Albert and his friends. Her first stop was the mayor's office where she asked for land for a ball field. After lecturing her about how women knew nothing about baseball, the mayor allowed Morhard to use two acres behind city hall and agreed to use city bulldozers to fix the field. Although money was tight, she convinced a sporting goods store to sell her bats, balls, and gloves at discounted prices. Eight boys ages nine to eleven joined Morhard's first team. She called them the Little Cleveland Indians.

But there was a problem: There were no teams to play. After some checking, she found a Catholic boys' team across town, and they played several games in the fall of 1937. Morhard, wearing a dress, high heel shoes, and a baseball cap perched on top of her bun, was both coach and umpire.

By the 1939 season, Morhard's league had eight teams who played a thirty-game schedule. She got permission from the Cleveland Indians owner, Alva Bradley, for the boys to wear uniforms just like the big-league teams, and she persuaded Cleveland Indian players to help coach the boys. Some of their sons even joined the league. In Morhard's league, every boy played at least one inning, and there was no cussing or arguing with umpires. If a player got out of line, she blew her whistle and stopped the game.

During the 1941 season, the Cleveland newspapers carried the boy's league box scores right below the Cleveland Indians box score. Everyone in Cleveland knew about the Little Indians, Little Yankees, Little White Sox and Little Cardinals. Hundreds of people attended the games.

On September 28, 1941, the Little World Series championship was attended by thousands and covered by most newspapers in the country. The Indians won 6-5. Morhard promised better things the following year.

However, two months later, the Japanese bombed Pearl Harbor and life changed in Cleveland. The league folded in 1944.

Over the years, Morhard received many calls about how to start a boy's baseball league. One such call came from Williamsport, Pennsylvania. Today, Williamsport is the home of the Little League World Series, but it is Josephine Morhard who established the first league. She got Albert off the street. He became an outstanding baseball player at Case Western University and a prominent trial lawyer in Cleveland. And Josephine Morhard became the mother of Little League Baseball.

REFERENCES

DeMarco, Laura. "How one Cleveland mom built a baseball league and brought Cleveland together." *The Plain Dealer,* September 19, 2019.

Morhard, Ruth Hanford. *Mrs. Morhard and the Boys; One Mother's Vision. The First Boys Baseball League. A Nation Inspired.* Plymouth: Citadel Publishing, May 26, 2020.

HANGING ON TO HOPE

"Oh, remember this; there is never a time when we may not hope in God. However great our difficulties, and though to all appearance help is impossible; yet our business is to hope in God, and it will be found that it is not in vain."
George Mueller

Monday, May 2, 2005 – Bridgeport, Connecticut: It was supposed to be an uneventful six-day sailing adventure to Bermuda on the 45-foot sailboat *Almeisan*. First mate Lochlin Reidy, age fifty-eight, had made sixteen crossings with Captain Tom Tighe. The captain had made the 600-mile trip 48 times. This one, at age sixty-five, was going to be his last. Also on board were three paying crewmembers, none of whom had sailing experience.

When the *Almeisan* left port, Tighe was aware of a low-pressure system that was forecasted to develop off the Georgia coast later in the week. He planned to sail east of the system and did not anticipate a problem. However, by Friday morning, the crew was encountering thirty-knot winds and ten-foot waves. It was too late to turn back. They couldn't outrun the storm. They had no choice but to sail through a rapidly strengthening low-pressure area off the North Carolina coast.

By Saturday afternoon, the *Almeisan* had dropped the sail and was trying to motor through twenty-foot seas as the storm intensified. At three a.m. Sunday morning, a 30-foot wave swamped the boat. With the boat damaged and taking on water, Tighe radioed the Coast Guard that they were abandoning the vessel. He turned on the emergency location beacon. Tighe and Reidy were deploying the lifeboat when a large wave knocked them both overboard. The other three crewmembers were left on the disabled boat.

Miraculously, the two men found each other amongst huge waves in the dark and tied their life jackets together with a short rope. They were in seventy-degree water and knew that if the storm did not drown them, hypothermia would probably kill them in twelve hours. The relentless waves often dunked them below the surface. Tighe saw the situation as hopeless. Reidy begged him to not give up. He promised the captain that he would get him home, but on Sunday afternoon Tighe died from hypothermia.

Committed to his promise, Reidy kept Tighe's body tethered to him. He had been in the water sixteen hours and wasn't sure how much longer he could hang on. His eyes were raw and his lips and tongue were severely swollen from the salt water. Reidy tried to focus on the positive—at least the storm was keeping the sharks below the surface.

On Sunday at five p.m., Reidy saw a Coast Guard C-130 plane drop out of the clouds. His hope was buoyed. The Coast Guard was searching for him, but then the plane was gone. As darkness fell, so did his hope. His teeth chattered, and his hands and feet were numb. Reidy wondered how he could he possibly make it through the night; finding a person in the Atlantic Ocean at night was virtually impossible.

Reidy convinced himself that if he could survive the night, the Coast Guard would find him at daylight. It was a speck of hope, but it was all he had. Occasionally, he removed a small strobe light from his lifejacket pocket and turned it on for thirty-minute intervals. Shortly after midnight, the C-130 was back. A spotter thought he saw a faint strobe light in the dark ocean below, but because of the heavy rain he could not be sure. The plane dropped flares to mark the spot and radioed the *Sakura Express*, an oil tanker that happened to be in the area, to help with the search.

The tanker located the flares and, after several minutes of shining a searchlight, got a brief glimpse of Reidy's orange life vest. As the ship rolled in thirty-foot seas, the crew performed a dramatic rescue. They lowered a cargo net and after several tries, Reidy was able to drag himself and the captain's stiff body into the net.

Against impossible odds, Lochlin Reidy's promise to his friend, Tom Tighe, had kept him hanging on when the situation seemed hopeless. He kept his promise. They were going home. On Sunday morning, a Coast Guard helicopter rescued the three crewmembers from the half-submerged *Almeisan*, and Reidy accompanied Tighe's body back to his family in Putnam Lake, New York.

REFERENCES

Murphy, Linda. "A Harrowing Tale: How Sailing Trip to Bermuda Turns into Nightmare." *The Herald News*, May 1, 2010.

Tougias, Michael J. *Overboard! A True Blue-water Odyssey of Disaster and Survival*. New York: Scribner Publishing Company, 2010.

WHEELCHAIR DREAMS

"Most people automatically assumed that because I had cerebral palsy, I could not or should not have pursued a coaching career. I was successful because I never listened to those people."
Doug Blevins

December 31, 1967 – Abingdon, Virginia: Five-year-old Doug Blevins and his father watched on TV as the Green Bay Packers beat the Dallas Cowboys in the inaugural NFL championship game—the coldest game in league history. On that cold Sunday in the foothills of the Blue Ridge Mountains, Doug started dreaming of being a football coach. And not just any coach, an NFL coach.

Doug's mother, Linda, figured his dream was a fleeting childhood fantasy, but the older he got, the more obsessed Doug became. Because he was born with cerebral palsy and would spend his life in a wheelchair, Linda knew the situation's likely outcome. She tried her best to steer Doug away from coaching, but she was unsuccessful.

When the small wheelchair-bound child talked about becoming a coach, teachers and friends smiled and nodded their heads. It was all Doug ever talked about. He wrote to every NFL head coach asking for coaching information. Doug's dream caught fire when Dallas Cowboy's Coach Tom Landry, the only coach to respond, sent a playbook and a coaching guide.

When he was a student at Abingdon High School, Doug started coaching the kickers. By then, he had read and watched everything he could find on kicking a football. Because of Doug's success, his story spread. After high school he landed an internship to work in the football department at the University of Tennessee under legendary coach Johnny Majors. Doug later transferred to East Tennessee State University where he worked with the kickers and pursued his dream.

In 1994, 31-year-old Doug landed a job with the New York Jets as a kicking adviser making $10,000 a year. The job didn't pay the bills, but Doug didn't care. He was in the NFL. In the off-season, he conducted kicking camps at his old high school to supplement his income.

Three years later, Miami Dolphins Coach Jimmy Johnson hired Doug, sight unseen, to be his kicking coach. When Doug arrived, Johnson assumed the young man in the motorized wheelchair was just another avid Dolphin's fan.

After two years with the Dolphins, Doug moved to the New England Patriots' coaching staff. While there, he received a video from a kicker at South Dakota State University, Adam Vinatieri, who dreamed of kicking in the NFL. Desperate for help, Vinatieri spent months in Abingdon with Doug. At the end of every practice session on the high school field, Vinatieri kicked a 48-yard field goal to "win the Super Bowl."

On February 3, 2002, Doug watched with tears in his eyes as Vinatieri booted a 48-yard field goal for the Patriots with six seconds left to beat the St. Louis Rams in the Super Bowl. Vinatieri's kick brought even more notoriety to Doug's unique ability to develop kickers. Soon parents across the country were bringing their children to Abingdon High School to be instructed by Doug.

During his four decades of coaching, Doug Blevins coached and mentored 26 former and current NFL kickers and punters. His list of kickers includes Vinatieri, the second-best kicker in NFL history, and Justin Tucker, the most accurate kicker in NFL history. In 2013, the kid who never kicked football and the first disabled coach was nominated for the NFL Hall of Fame.

Today, 58-year-old Doug Blevins is the kicking coach at East Tennessee State University, his alma mater. He still runs his own kicking consulting company. In his office are Super Bowl-winning footballs, an NFL Hall of Fame nomination, awards from high school and college kickers, and other football memorabilia. Those who dream of punting or kicking in college, or the NFL, come from all over the world to learn kicking lessons at Doug's wheelchair.

REFERENCES

Avento, Joe. "Disability Doesn't Keep ETSU's Blevins from the Top of his Profession." *Johnson City Press*, March 9, 2021,

Carpenter, Les. "The Man in a Wheelchair Who Helped Kick off a Super Bowl Dynasty." ThePostGame.com, February 2, 2012. https://www.thepostgame.com/blog/good-sports/201202/man-wheelchair-who-helped-kick-super-bowl-dynasty.

Ervin, Mike. "Kicking Coach Doug Blevins Creates Champions from His Chair." Abilities.com, Accessed March 31, 2022. https://www.abilities.com/community/adaptive-sports-kicking-coach.html.

Klemko, Robert. "Kicking Guru Doug Blevins Shocked by Hall of Fame Nomination." *USA Today*, October 7, 2012.

DREAM BIG—DARE TO FAIL

"A man is not old until his regrets take the place of dreams."
John Barrymore

1927 – Harvard University – Cambridge, Massachusetts: Norman Vaughn read the headlines of the Boston newspaper: "Byrd to the South Pole." The 22-year-old Harvard student was trying to make the freshman football team, but thoughts of the expedition intrigued him.

He told his four roommates, "I've got to do this!" They all laughed, but they knew that he had dropped out of Harvard three years earlier and used sled dogs to deliver medical supplies in Labrador. Vaughan was drawn to things that would cause others to run away.

The following day, Vaughan showed up at Richard Byrd's home in Boston to sign up for the expedition, but the maid refused to let him speak to the Admiral. Vaughn tracked down W.A. McDonald, the journalist who had written the article and convinced him to send

Byrd the message: "I have sled dog driving experience in Labrador. I will leave Harvard to go to New Hampshire to assemble and train your 100 dogs. I will do all of this for no pay."

After eleven months of Vaughan's persistence, Byrd accepted his offer and Vaughan dropped out of Harvard a second time for a mission to explore the South Pole. In the summer of 1928, Vaughan was part of the team that established Little America, Byrd's basecamp on the Antarctic's Ross Ice Shelf. His well-prepared husky sled teams helped in the successful mapping of the polar region. Admiral Byrd was so pleased with Vaughan's contribution that he named a 10,300-foot mountain, "Mount Vaughan."

In 1932, Vaughan represented the United States in the winter Olympics in Lake Placid, New York—the only time dog sledding was a demonstration sport in the Olympics. Later, during World War II, his dog sled ambulance teams rescued American soldiers in Germany, France, and Belgium. After the war, Vaughn became chief of search and rescue for the International Civil Aviation Organization.

In 1971, at age sixty-five, Norman Vaughn moved to Alaska. The next year he participated in his first Iditarod Sled Dog Race which at almost 1,200 miles is Alaska's longest and most grueling dog race. He participated in the event thirteen times before race organizers kicked him out for being too old and slow.

On the day that Admiral Byrd named the mountain for him, Vaughan told Byrd, "One day I will come back and climb it," to which Byrd had replied, "Norman, I believe you will." It was an opportunity that Vaughan dreamed about for more than sixty years. At age eighty-seven, he decided to finally climb his mountain to celebrate his 88th birthday.

Vaughan raised more than a million dollars to fund the expedition, no small thing for a man approaching ninety. When one of the expedition's supply planes crashed on takeoff for Antarctica, the expedition had to be canceled. Friends and family suggested that Vaughan scrap the mission, but he responded, "Dream big—dare to fail." It had become the theme of Vaughan's life and not the first time the family had heard these words.

In 1994, on his 89th birthday, Norman Vaughan reached the summit of Mount Vaughan, the mountain Admiral Byrd had named for him 65 years earlier. National Geographic accompanied the team to capture the story. But Vaughan wasn't done yet. In 1997, at age 92, he created his own dog sled race: the 800-mile Norm Vaughan Serum Run from Nenana to Nome, Alaska.

Norman Vaughan died December 19, 2005, four days after his 100th birthday. At the time of his death, he had been in the early planning stages of a return to Antarctica for a second climb of his mountain.

REFERENCES

Andrews, Andy. *Storms of Perfection, Volume 3*. Lightning Crown, February 6, 2013.

Gillespie, Elgy. "Mister Sled." *The Guardian,* May 17, 2005.

"Norman Vaughan." Alaska Sports Hall Of Fame, February 24, 2016. https://alaskasportshall.org/inductee/norman-vaughan/.

Saxon, Wolfgang. "Norman Dane Vaughan, Antarctic Explorer, Dies at 100." The New York Times, December 22, 2005.

Snow, Crocker. "Chasing Down a Legend: The Story of Colonel Norman Vaughan." *Alaskan Dispatch,* September 30, 2016.

THE MASONIC HOME MIGHTY MITES

"Why do we automatically assume that someone who is smaller or poorer or less skilled is necessarily at a disadvantage? Underdogs win all the time. The very thing that gives the giant his size is often the source of his greatest weakness."
Malcolm Gladwell

1926 - Masonic Home and School, Ft. Worth, Texas: The Masonic Home Orphanage, which sat on 200 acres just east of Ft. Worth, Texas, was started in 1900 for the purpose of housing and educating the orphans of Free Masons. The facility, a lonely, depressing place, was home for 150 children, including five-year-old Hardy Brown and his two siblings who were sent to live at the home after witnessing their father be gunned down by a rival bootlegger.

The Ft. Worth Masonic Home never had a football team until they hired Rusty Russell in the summer of 1927 as the school's first coach. The young coach wasn't sure why he took the job. He was having great success as the coach of the Temple High School Wildcats having taken them to the state semi-finals the previous year. Fellow coaches deemed Russell crazy to leave a well-established Texas program and his very pregnant wife agreed. No one believed the tiny orphanage could ever compete in high school football, but Russell ignored his head and followed his heart.

In 1927, the Masonic Home Masons played in the B division, the smallest division in Texas. Russell hauled his team to away games in a smoke-belching flatbed truck. Though the twelve players in donated, mismatched uniforms and hand-me-down helmets didn't look like much, they shocked the Texas football world by going 8-2 in their first season. After watching the team play a sportswriter dubbed the speedy, undersized boys the "Mighty Mites" and so they were.

Russell's offense, an early version of the spread offense, utilized the speed and quickness of players often outweighed by fifty pounds per man. From 1927 to 1931, the orphans compiled a 37-11 record. Texas had never seen this style of gritty, relentless football. Bound by death and hardship, the boys were determined to prove to the world that they were somebody.

In 1932, the Mighty Mites moved up to Class 7A, the largest football division in Texas. With twelve players—all who could fit on the old truck—they competed against schools with several thousand students who dressed out a hundred players. They routinely beat the big, rich schools in Dallas, Houston, and Amarillo. These teams quickly learned to fear the hard-hitting Mighty Mites who had nothing to lose and everything to prove.

The Mighty Mites reached the state semi-finals in 1934, 1938, and 1940. With All-State Linebacker Hardy Brown, they played three-time state champion Amarillo High in the 1940 state championship game. After being stopped on the one-yard-line as time ran out, the Mighty Mites lost a heart breaker 14-7 to the Golden Sandies. The twelve orphans walked off the field as 12,000 fans stood to their feet chanting "Mighty Mites! Mighty Mites!"

Although the Mighty Mites never won a championship, they captured the hearts of millions of people in Texas and across America. In 1940, the city of Ft. Worth built a 15,000-seat stadium to accommodate the Mighty Mite crowds. The stadium became known as "The House the Orphans Built."

Rusty Russell coached fifteen years at the Masonic Home, compiling a 127-30-12 record. He was later the head coach at Southern Methodist University and, in 1971, was inducted into the Texas High School Football Hall of Fame.

After graduating from the Masonic School in 1940, Hardy Brown signed a scholarship with the University of Tulsa where he was All Missouri Valley Conference linebacker for three years. The 6-foot, 190-pound Brown played for 10 seasons in the National Football League with the Baltimore Colts, San Francisco 49ers, and Washington Redskins. Hardy Brown ranks number five on the Top 10 Hardest Hitters in NFL History list.

Eighty years later, people still talk about the underdog kids from a tiny orphanage in Texas who traveled to games on an old flatbed truck. Rusty Russell gave the orphans two things they desperately needed: hope and an opportunity to be something other than orphans. They were winners!

REFERENCES

Dent, Jim. *Twelve Mighty Orphans: The Inspiring True Story of the Mighty Mites Who Ruled* Texas Football. New York: Thomas Dunne Books, September 4, 2007.

O'Donnell, Bob. "The Most Dangerous Player Who Ever Buckled a Chinstrap." www.profootballdaily.com.

"Rusty Russell (American Football Coach)." Wikipedia. Wikimedia Foundation, January 4, 2022. https://en.wikipedia.org/wiki/Rusty_Russell_(American_football_coach).

SIX MINUTES THAT STUNNED THE WORLD

"When life takes the wind out of your sails, it is time to test the oars."
Robert Brault

September 1935 – Seattle, Washington: University of Washington crew coach Al Ulbrickson told the Seattle Times that his Huskies would win the gold medal in the 1936 Olympics eight-man crew event or he would quit his job. It was an extraordinary boast from a coach who had never won a NCAA championship and never even been to the Olympics.

In America in the 1930s, collegiate rowing was almost as popular as basketball and football. On the West Coast, the University of California-Berkeley and the University of Washington dominated the sport while Harvard, Yale, and Princeton were East Coast powers. It was common for 100,000 people to watch a crew competition.

During the first competition of the 1936 season, Ulbrickson knew he had the right mix of power, endurance, and teamwork in the boat when his team beat rival and highly favored Cal-Berkeley, and he hoped this perfect combination would take him to Berlin. On June 22 in New York, Washington out rowed Cal and the best East Coast teams to capture the national championship. Two weeks later, the underdog Huskies beat out six competing boats, including several veteran teams, to win the Olympic trial.

On July 14, the U.S. Olympic team left New York on a steamship bound for Germany. Germany was the odds-makers favorite to win the Olympic rowing events. True to prediction, the Germans dominated their six Olympics rowing events preceding the final event, the men's eight-oared race, winning five gold and a silver medal.

On the morning of August 14, people in Western Washington woke up excited to listen to the nine a.m. radio coverage of the eight-man crew event. For the first time, NBC and CBS were carrying Olympic events live nationwide.

In Germany, Don Hume, the Huskies most important rower, whose stroke set the pace for the boat, was so sick with high fever and chills that he couldn't get out of bed. Ulbrickson had no choice but to replace him in the boat. However, team members appealed the decision and convinced the coach that they would cover for Hume.

At race time, it was raining and windy on the lake, and to further stack the odds against them, the U.S. team was assigned to lane six, the lane with most exposure to the head wind. The Germans, to no one's surprise, drew the calmer lane one. Then, the American team failed to hear or see the starter drop his flag and got a late start in the 2,000-meter race.

At 600 meters, the Americans were almost two boat lengths behind the lead boat, Italy. At the halfway point, they were dead last, a full five seconds behind the Italians, with Germany in second place. At 1,200 meters, Hume, battling exhaustion, picked up the pace to 32 strokes per minute and with 500 meters to go, the American boat was dead even with the Germans and Italians.

Adolf Hitler was on his feet as 75,000 Germans, the largest crowd to ever see a rowing event in Europe, thundered "Deutsch-land, Deutsch-land, Deutsch-land." At 1,800 meters, Hume and his teammates, rowing past the pain and the little voices in their heads that said what they were trying to do was impossible, took the stroke to a dangerous, heart-bursting level of 44 strokes per minute. The three boats remained neck-and-neck-and-neck.

When the boats crossed the finish line, it was difficult to determine the winner from the stands. Hitler, thinking the Germans were victorious, stood with his clenched fist raised in the air. After a long pause, the announcement came over the loudspeaker: USA 6 minutes, 25.4 seconds, Italy 6:26.0, Germany 6:26.4 seconds. The roar of the crowd faded quickly. The University of Washington had done the impossible.

Jesse Owens stole the 1936 Olympic U.S. newspaper headlines by winning four gold medals in track and field, but in Seattle, the biggest sports news of the century occurred on a lake in Grenau, Germany, on August 14, 1936, when a group of nine college boys shocked the Germans and stunned the world by winning the eight-man crew competition.

REFERENCES

"A Tribute to Bob Moch & 1936 Olympic Team." Huskeycrew.com. January 23, 2005.

Brown, Daniel James. *The Boys in the Boat.* New York: Penguin Books, May 2014.

Socolow, Michael J. *Six Minutes in Berlin.* Champaign: UI Press, November 14, 2016.

MR. UNIVERSE

"When you set out to do something great, most people will not see what you see... don't allow their version of how your life should turn out to affect you. You will have to do what they are not willing to do."
Andy Andrews

October 24, 1965 – Graz, Austria: He tossed and turned in his military bunk. It was going to be another sleepless night for the eighteen-year-old serving his one-year of mandatory service in the Austrian army. The Junior Mr. Europe bodybuilding championship was a week away in Stuttgart, Germany, but how could he compete? The army scoffed at his bodybuilding dream. They would not grant him leave to travel to Germany.

Arnold Schwarzenegger was born in Thal, Austria, in 1947. His father, a former member of the Nazi party, was the police chief in the small town, and he thought his son should become a policeman too. His mother thought Arnold should get a trade, like carpentry, because he did poorly in school.

At age fourteen, Arnold saw a bodybuilding magazine with Mr. Universe Reg Park on the cover. He dreamed of being Mr. Universe and of becoming the strongest man in the world. To his father's embarrassment, Arnold quit soccer and was the only kid in town who lifted weights.

As Arnold lay in his bunk, he considered going AWOL from the Army, even though he knew there would be severe discipline if caught. Maybe he was crazy even to consider entering the Mr. Europe event. The Austrian Army was trying to make a tank driver out of him. Arnold had other plans. He would someday get to America, become the strongest man in the world, star in movies, be a millionaire, and, one day, he would be in politics.

Should he go AWOL and try to get to Stuttgart? Would he even be able to get there? Should he give up on this whole crazy idea? His father had told him that he was ashamed of him. His friends laughed at his passion for lifting weights for endless hours, and the Army thought he was nuts.

A few nights later, Arnold snuck out of the barracks. He jumped a freight train and rode twenty-six hours to Stuttgart. Upon arriving at the competition, he had to borrow another competitor's gym trunks to compete. When Arnold returned to the army base, he spent a week in solitary confinement, but it was worth it. He had won the 1965 Junior Mr. Europe Bodybuilding Championship.

After his week in solitary, the base commander called Schwarzenegger to his office. He interrogated the soldier at length about the incident, but at the conclusion, the senior officer asked, "So, you won the Mr. Europe Competition?" A few days later, Schwarzenegger was transferred from tank driver to cook so he could get the best food.

The base commander had weightlifting equipment built for his new champion, and he re-arranged Mr. Europe's daily schedule so that he had four hours to work out. Schwarzenegger had the big break that he could have never imagined possible.

In 1967, twenty-year-old Arnold Schwarzenegger shocked the bodybuilding world when he won the Amateur Mr. Universe competition in London. A year later, he moved to California and captured another Mr. Universe competition. Additional Mr. Universe titles followed in 1969 and 1970.

Schwarzenegger is the only bodybuilder to win the professional Mr. Olympia contest six times in a row (1970-75) before retiring. He has starred in twenty-eight movies, with his appearances in *The Terminator* being the most memorable. His net worth today is an estimated $400 million. And Schwarzenegger served two terms as California's governor from 2004-12.

Arnold Schwarzenegger believed in a dream that no one else saw. He says, "I knew that bodybuilding was the perfect choice for me. No one else seemed to agree—especially my family and friends. To them, the only acceptable career was to take some established job. My dream to build my body and become Mr. Universe was totally beyond their comprehension."

REFERENCES

"Arnold Schwarzenegger." Biography.com. A&E Networks Television, April 12, 2021. https://www.biography.com/actor/arnold-schwarzenegger.

"Arnold Schwarzenegger: Biography." Arnold Schwarzenegger. Accessed March 31, 2022. http://www.schwarzenegger.com/bio.

"Arnold Schwarzenegger." Encyclopedia Britannica. Encyclopedia Britannica, inc. Accessed March 31, 2022. https://www.britannica.com/biography/Arnold-Schwarzenegger.

COACH

"We will all be confronted with some adversity that seems insurmountable and we will have a choice. We can feel sorry for ourselves and make everyone around us miserable, or we can, with God's help, become stronger and make a difference."
Charlie Wedemeyer

December 1984 – Los Gatos, California: Coach's death seemed imminent. His 95- pound frame clung to life support in his bedroom. Ramona, one of his nurses, felt impressed to lay hands on him and pray. As she did, Coach felt a jolt of power flow through him. A wilted amaryllis plant next to the bed suddenly bloomed, and he was able to eat two bowls of soup—more than he had eaten in two weeks. He and his wife Lucy became Christians that night.

Charlie Wedemeyer was born and raised on the island of Oahu, Hawaii. The 5-foot-7-inch quarterback was voted the best high school football player in Hawaii during the decade of the sixties. In 1975, after a successful football career at Michigan State University, he married Lucy Dangler, his high school sweetheart, and got a job coaching football at Los Gatos High School in California.

In February 1978, a few months after becoming the high school's head coach, thirty-year-old Wedemeyer was diagnosed with Lou Gehrig's disease. Doctors told him he would live a year. Lucy told him, "This isn't your disease, Charlie. It's our disease. Whatever happens we will face it together."

Los Gatos won back-to-back conference championships in 1978 and 1979. By then, Coach had difficulty gripping chalk, and after several falls down the steps at school, the school principal moved his classroom to the ground floor. Lucy was shaving him and driving him to school. In 1980, Coach was voted conference coach of the year after winning a third straight championship. The principal did not renew Coach's teaching contract but allowed him to continue to coach.

By the 1982 football season, Coach was in a wheelchair, but used a golf cart during games. His team was 9-1 and won their fifth conference championship. Lucy drove the golf cart the following season. At that point, Coach had difficulty speaking so Lucy used signs to relay the plays to an assistant coach.

In the spring of 1985, a few months after Coach's salvation, Lucy asked his doctors to place him on a ventilator and remove his "Do Not Resuscitate" status. The doctors were opposed. "Charlie has already beaten the odds. He should give up and die." Lucy got her way and the ventilator had immediate results; Coach no longer struggled to breathe and could sleep through the night.

Next came the feeding tube. Coach began to gain weight. On life support, with Lucy at his side calling plays, he once again coached the 1985 season from his golf cart, and Los Gatos won the California Central Coast Championship. After the season, Los Gatos demoted Coach to coach the freshman team the following season. It was okay with him because it allowed him more time for the speaking requests that flooded his mailbox.

With Lucy reading his lips and delivering his speeches, Coach spoke at churches, schools, at Folsom Prison, and to scientists at NASA. "I believe it's not our responsibility to know why," Coach told audiences, "But to trust that God has a reason and purpose for everything that happens to us. And He can salvage good out of any circumstance."

In July 2007, Charlie Wedemeyer was inducted into the National High School Football Hall of Fame. He died three years later, on June 3, 2010, more than three decades after his initial diagnosis. Several thousand former players, family, friends, and celebrities attended the 64-year-old coach's memorial service at Calvary Church in Los Gatos. They came to celebrate the life of a warrior. A fighter. A guy who refused to give up despite the odds.

REFERENCES

Emmons, Mark. "Charlie Wedemeyer's inspirational memorial service—full of laughter, tinged with tears." *Mercury News.* June 19, 2010.

Farmer, Sam. "Charlie Wedemeyer dies at 64; high school football coach inspired many in battle with Lou Gehrig's disease." *Los Angeles Times*, June 5, 2010.

"The Herman Wedemeyer Home Page." The Herman Wedemeyer Home Page. Accessed March 31, 2022. http://www.wedey.usanethosting.com/.

Wedemeyer, Charlie and Lucy. *Charlie's Victory.* Grand Rapids: Zondervan Publishing, March 1, 1993.

AT ROCK BOTTOM

"There was never a night or problem that could defeat sunrise or hope."
Bernard Williams

2:45 p.m. Saturday, April 26, 2003 – Blue John Canyon, Utah: Aron Ralston had hiked seven miles into Blue John Canyon and was climbing over an eight-foot boulder when the 1,000-pound rock suddenly shifted, pinning his right wrist between the rock and the canyon wall. He struggled for several minutes to yank his arm free, but he was trapped.

The 27-year-old seasoned mountain climber had planned to be back at his truck, eight miles away, before dark. Aron was wedged between the rocks in such a way that he couldn't even sit down. Because he had violated a cardinal rule of wilderness travel and told no one of his specific travel plans, no one knew where he was. Aron realized that it was not his hand that he needed to worry about—it was his life.

The boulder had Aron's wrist pinned so tightly that there was no bleeding. In his backpack, he had two bean burritos and only twenty-two ounces of water. He knew the average survival time in the desert without water was roughly three days and figured he could survive until Tuesday or Wednesday. But the chances that another hiker might find him in the remote canyon would be like winning the lottery.

Aron thought about amputating his arm at the wrist. In his backpack, he had a utility tool with a dull knife blade. But how would he saw through the bones? Would he bleed to death in the process? Did he have the courage to do it?

After twelve hours of standing, Aron figured out how to use his climbing ropes to fashion a swing seat with his free hand. The swing took a little of the load off his legs. Sleeping was virtually impossible. With temperatures in the low 50s, Aron shivered through the long first night clad only in shorts and a t-shirt.

The Sunday morning sun brought hope. Maybe somebody would come along today. But by late Monday afternoon, Aron's hope was almost gone. Trapped for fifty-two hours, his water gone, Aron faced a second long night in the canyon.

Aron began to save his urine in the water bottle to have some form of liquid to drink. By Tuesday morning, believing it was his only chance for survival, Aron decided to try to cut his arm off. Using his knife, he began the painful process, but after sawing for a few minutes, he realized he didn't have the stomach to do it.

By Wednesday morning, any hope of being found alive was gone. After ninety-six hours of sleep deprivation and exposure, Aron was hallucinating and shivering uncontrollably from cold and fatigue. He carved his epitaph on the rock and hoped to die in the next twenty-four hours. The weather had gotten colder, and he was confident he wouldn't last another night.

Thursday morning dawned, not with, "Great, I'm alive," but, "Oh, I'm still here." Aron noticed insects swarming at his wrist, drawn to the rotting flesh. Suddenly, it occurred to him that if he torqued his arm far enough, he might be able to break the bones. Standing, he applied pressure first to snap the radius and then the ulna bone, which popped like a rifle shot. He used the knife blade to cut through the ligaments and tendons above his right wrist. The gory process took almost two hours.

On Thursday at 11:30 a.m., Aron Ralston was finally free of the rock that had held him prisoner for almost five days. After applying a tourniquet, he started the long walk to his truck. Near his vehicle, he met three hikers who called for help. He was transported to a hospital by a helicopter.

After adjusting to a prosthetic arm, Aron returned to canyoneering and mountain climbing. According to Aron, "The tragedy inspired me to test myself. You'll never find your limits until you've gone too far." Today he has climbed 47 of the 59 Colorado mountain peaks taller than 14,000 feet.

REFERENCES

"Aron Ralston." Wikipedia. Wikimedia Foundation, March 22, 2022. https://en.wikipedia.org/wiki/Aron_Ralston.

Ralston, Aron. *Between a Rock and a Hard Place*. New York: Simon & Schuster, August 2005.

Speik, Robert. "Solo Climber Aron Ralston Forced to Amputate His Arm." Traditionalmountaineering.com, May 2, 2003. http://www.traditionalmountaineering.org/News_Lost_Solo.htm.

ALONE IN THE ATLANTIC

"He had no ability to give up. It wasn't that he didn't want to quit, he couldn't. It wasn't in him. It never had been."
Dan Groat

April 1, 1982 – Boston, Massachusetts: The phone call, the one the family had dreaded, came late afternoon. The U.S. Coast Guard called to inform the parents of Steven Callahan that the search in the North Atlantic Ocean for their son's missing sailboat had been canceled. The Callahan's begged the Coast Guard to continue the search to no avail. The family knew that the chances of survival were virtually zero, however they refused to give up hope.

That same day, thirty-year-old Steven Callahan continued to drift westward across the Atlantic in a small raft. It had been fifty-six days since his sailboat sunk. Only a handful of people in history had survived this long while lost at sea.

From the time Steven Callahan was twelve, he dreamed of sailing solo across the Atlantic Ocean. In

1981, he built a 21-foot sailboat, *Napoleon Solo*, and sailed it from Rhode Island to Bermuda to England. On January 29, 1982, Steven began the return crossing from the Canary Islands to Antigua in the West Indies.

During a storm on the night of February 4, Steven was jolted out of sleep by a terrific crash. A whale had damaged his boat. As water flooded into the cabin, he inflated the nylon raft. Steven was able to salvage an emergency kit containing about two weeks of food, a few flares, a spear gun, and a solar still for making drinking water. He figured if he could survive for three months, he might reach Antigua or Guadeloupe by late April. It was his only hope.

Following the Coast Guard phone call, Steven's family vowed to continue the search. Steven's father, who had flown search and rescue missions in the military, knew the Atlantic intimately. He assumed that Steven capsized during the storm on February 4. He plotted two probable drift patterns for the raft using two possible sailing routes Steven would have taken. One of the two possible positions he calculated was within 100 miles of Steven's position.

After Steven's food supply ran out, his diet consisted of the occasional triggerfish or dolphin he could spear. Clumps of Sargasso weed containing tiny shrimp, fish, and crabs also provided food. Although he was slowly starving, the worst part of the ordeal was that the solar still could only produce 16-18 ounces of drinking water each day. Steven drifted on an endless ocean and constantly dreamed of food, water, and home.

Steven often thought about suicide. He was tempted to quit fighting for survival. It would be so easy to give up; he could drink salt water and die of a swollen tongue from thirst, or fall overboard and be eaten by sharks. But he refused to let go of the hope that land was just over the horizon.

On April 6, Steven spotted ship number seven on the horizon, just a couple of miles away. His hope soared. He shot one of his three remaining flares into the air but got no response. His body cried "quit," but his spirit said "no." His back, his butt, and his legs were now scabbed over with large salt-water boils from constant rubbing against the raft.

Two weeks later, day seventy-six in the raft, three fishermen noticed birds circling and discovered a small raft bobbing in the ocean a few miles off the coast of Guadeloupe. To their astonishment, they found an emaciated 110-pound Steven Callahan, still clinging to hope, having drifted 1,800 miles across the Atlantic Ocean.

Now more than thirty years later, Steven Callahan is an editor for two sailing magazines, designs sailboats, and sails every chance that he gets. "To this day I feel my experience has given me a strange kind of wealth, the most important kind. I value each moment," says the veteran sailor. "I don't regret my 76 days alone in the raft."

REFERENCES

Callahan, Steven. *Adrift.* Boston: Mariner Books, October 17, 2002.

"Steve Callahan Writer, Best-Selling Author of Adrift, Sailor, Speaker, Boat Designer, Consultant on Survival, Seamanship, and Marine Services." Steve Callahan Writer, Best-Selling Author of Adrift, Sailor, Speaker, Boat Designer, Consultant on Survival, Seamanship, and Marine Services." Accessed March 31, 2022. http://www.stevencallahan.net/.

"Steven Callahan." Wikipedia. Wikimedia Foundation, March 14, 2022. https://en.wikipedia.org/wiki/Steven_Callahan.

THE FAT KID

"How it is, isn't how it has to be—it is simply how it is right now. Your possibilities are as limitless as your dreams."
James Richardson

August 1994 – University of Arkansas, Fayetteville, Arkansas: After practice, Arkansas Head Football Coach Danny Ford asked recruiting coach Harold Horton, "Who is that fat kid?" Ford was informed that the 6-foot-2-inch, 310-pound freshman walk-on guard was Brandon Burlsworth from Harrison, Arkansas. Ford shook his head, "Hell, he won't ever make it!" Horton responded, "Coach, Burlsworth's older brother Marty called me almost every day about a walk-on spot for him…he was 3A All-State… and Coach, he has a big heart."

Brandon Burlsworth was born in 1976 in Harrison, Arkansas, in the foothills of the Ozark Mountains. His parents divorced when he was two leaving his mom to raise him and two teenage brothers. Brandon learned how to call the hogs—Arkansas Razorback style—and, as a child, dreamed of one day wearing the red razorback jersey.

As a six-foot, 160-pound sophomore guard, Brandon drew lots of laughs and nasty comments from his high school teammates at Harrison High when he announced in the locker room that he was going to play football at the University of Arkansas. At the time, he didn't even start for the Golden Goblins.

By his junior year Brandon had gained 80 pounds. He started that season at guard and earned all-district honors. The coach opened the weight room every morning at 6:15 a.m. so Brandon could lift weights before school. As a senior, he stood 6-foot-2-inches, weighed 300 pounds, and made the all-state team.

When Marty began to call Coach Horton about a scholarship for his younger brother, Horton was emphatic, "Good high school size, but too small and too slow for division one football. Try a smaller college." Three Arkansas small colleges, including Ouachita Baptist University, were interested, but his little brother dreamed of playing for the Razorbacks. Marty began to pester Horton about a walk-on opportunity and finally wore him down.

During Brandon's freshman season at Arkansas, he dropped 60 pounds of fat and added 60 pounds of muscle to reshape his body into a 6-foot-3-inch, 310-pound division one lineman body. As a sophomore, he earned the scholarship he had long dreamed about and started at right guard. His junior year he was voted first-team All-Southeastern Conference guard.

Houston Nutt became the new head coach at Arkansas before Brandon's senior year in 1998. One night when leaving his office around nine p.m., Nutt heard someone in the weight room and discovered Brandon working out. Nutt coined the term "Do it Burls Way" as the team motto. Brandon helped lead the Razorbacks to a 9-3 season that year and was voted All-SEC and All-American.

Brandon Burlsworth ran the fastest 40-yard time, 4.88, ever run by a lineman at the National Football League combine. In April 1999, the Baltimore Colts drafted him in the third round—the first guard taken in the draft. They planned to start him at right guard as a rookie.

On Wednesday, April 28, eleven days after the NFL draft, Brandon was driving from Fayetteville to Harrison to go to church with his mother. He was killed in a head-on collision with an 18-wheeler a few miles from home. That fall, Arkansas retired Brandon Burlsworth's jersey number 77, only the second jersey to ever be retired by the school.

After his death, family and friends created the Brandon Burlsworth Foundation to honor Brandon's work ethic and Christian values. The foundation buys thirty tickets to each Arkansas home game to give underprivileged children a chance to attend games. It also provides eighteen scholarships annually to students from small towns in Arkansas.

In 2013, *Bleacher Report* voted Brandon Burlsworth the greatest walk-on of the BCS football era. Each year, the Burlsworth trophy is presented to the top college football walk-on. Today, in the corner of the Razorback locker room sits Brandon Burlsworth's football locker with his helmet and jersey. It is encased in glass with a sign above it which reads, "Do it Burls Way"—a silent reminder to all who pass to never give up on their dreams.

REFERENCES

"Burlsworth Football Camps." The BBF. Accessed March 31, 2022. http://www.brandonburlsworth.org/.

Foxsports. "The Life and Still-Impactful Legacy of Brandon Burlsworth." FOX Sports. FOX Sports, February 17, 2016. https://www.foxsports.com/stories/college-football/the-life-and-still-impactful-legacy-of-brandon-burlsworth.

"Grant Morgan (American Football)." Wikipedia. Wikimedia Foundation, March 10, 2022. https://en.wikipedia.org/wiki/Grant_Morgan_(American_football).

"2021 Trophy Winner Grant Morgan." Burlsworth Trophy. Accessed March 31, 2022. http://www.burlsworthtrophy.com/.

THE MOMENT THAT SAVED A CAREER

"I was just trying to make the world a little bit better. That's what you are supposed to do with your life, isn't it?"
Pee Wee Reese

July 1918: Harry Peter Henry "Pee Wee" Reese was born in Ekron, Kentucky. He was so small that he did not start on his high school baseball team. In 1938 he was playing in a church league where the local minor league baseball team, the Louisville Colonels, discovered him and offered him $200 to sign a contract.

Two years later Reese made the major league at shortstop for the Brooklyn Dodgers. In 1942 he played in his first all-star game and went on to make the all-star team for ten straight years. In 1984 he was selected into the Baseball Hall of Fame.

In January 1919, Jack Roosevelt "Jackie" Robinson was born in Cairo, Georgia, to a family of sharecroppers. His father left home when he was six months old and then his mother moved the family to Pasadena, California, to be near relatives. An all-around athlete, he became the first student at UCLA to win varsity letters in four sports: baseball, football, basketball, and track.

In 1945 white professional sports were not available to Black athletes. So, after being discharged from the Army, Robinson signed to play for the Kansas City Monarchs in the Negro Baseball League. After his first season, Robinson was shocked to get a phone call from Branch Rickey, the Brooklyn Dodgers manager, with a contract offer.

Rickey, who believed the time had come to integrate baseball, said to him, "Jackie, there's virtually nobody on our side. No owner, no umpires, very few newspapermen. I'm afraid that many fans may be hostile. We'll be in a tough position, but we can do this."

On April 14, 1947 at Washington Park in Brooklyn, New York, the opening day of the Major League Baseball season, Robinson made his debut at first base for the Brooklyn Dodgers, making him the first Black man to ever play in a big league game. It had been tough. In spring training, several teammates had quit rather than play with him. He took the field to the sound of boos and racial catcalls from the hometown crowd. Off the field, Robinson and his wife Rachel received death threats.

On May 13, 1947, the second road trip of the season found the Dodgers visiting the Cincinnati Reds at Crosley Field. Early in the game, Robinson had made two errors and the opposing fans were booing and taunting him unmercifully when Pee Wee Reese, the Dodgers team captain and all-star shortstop, called timeout.

After glaring for a long moment at the fans, he walked over to Robinson at first base, stood beside him, and put his arm around him. The ballpark grew eerily quiet. Reese shook the young player's hand and slowly walked back to shortstop. For the rest of the game, fans cheered each time that Robinson came to the plate.

Robinson played in 154 games that first season and thought about giving up after most of them. But he realized the stage was bigger than he was, so he refused to quit. At the end of that first season, Robinson won the "Sporting News Rookie of the Year" award in the National League. Two years later, he earned the league's "Most Valuable Player" award. Robinson led the Dodgers to six World Series appearances before retiring in 1956. In 1962, he was voted into the Major League Baseball Hall of Fame.

Jackie Robinson never forgot that moment in April 1947. "Pee Wee Reese made me feel like I belonged in the big leagues," he later recalled, "That one moment may have saved my career." In 1997, to celebrate the 50th anniversary of Robinson's first season, every team in Major League Baseball permanently retired his number 42. He is the only major league player to have ever earned this distinction.

REFERENCES

Berkow, Ira. "Two Men Who Did the Right Thing." *New York Times,* November 2, 2005.

Cronin, Brian. "Did Reese Really Embrace Robinson in '47?" ESPN, April 15, 2013.

Fitzpatrick, Frank. "A Civil Rights Monument, Jackie Robinson's Debut Changed the Face of Baseball." *Philadelphia Inquirer,* April 16, 2017.

"Steeplechase Park - Jackie Robinson and Pee Wee Reese Monument: NYC Parks." Steeplechase Park Monuments. Accessed March 31, 2022. https://www.nycgovparks.org/parks/steeplechase-park/monuments/1982.

MR. ACCURACY

"Life's challenges are not supposed to paralyze you; they're supposed to help you discover who you are."
Bernice Johnson Reagon

1956 – St. Louis, Missouri: Calvin Peete was in terrible pain. The 12-year-old had fallen out of a tree at his grandmother's house and landed on his arm. The x-ray showed his left elbow was fractured in three places. The physician recommended surgery, but there was no money for that. After advising Calvin's grandmother who, after his parent's divorce had become his primary caretaker, that the elbow could be stiff and crooked when it healed, the doctor put a cast on his arm. The doctor was right.

Calvin's father remarried a year after the accident and moved to Pahokee, Florida, and Calvin went to live with him. He dropped out of school in the 8th grade and joined his father picking fruits and vegetables in the hot sun—a job he hated worse than school.

At eighteen, Calvin convinced his grandmother to help him buy a Plymouth station wagon. He got a peddler's license; stocked the car with watches, jewelry, and clothing; and started selling to migrant workers in Florida. As a sideline, he made spending money by hustling in pool halls and playing poker. By the mid-1960s, Calvin had peddled his goods up the East Coast and settled in upstate New York.

One afternoon Calvin thought he and his three buddies were going to a clambake but, to his surprise, they stopped at Genesee Valley Golf Course in Rochester, New York. His friends gave him two choices: play in their foursome or sit in the car. "Who wants to chase a stupid golf ball under the hot sun," the 23-year-old Calvin asked. "It's a silly game…" But he rented a set of clubs.

His first round of golf was comical to his friends and frustrating to Calvin—until late in the round when he birdied a hole. He fell in love with a sport he thought was only played by sissies and rich white people. When his buddies left the golf course, Calvin went to the practice range. He hit golf balls well past the blisters until it was too dark to see.

Golf captivated Calvin's life. Within six months, his scores were in the low 80s, and after a year, he was a par golfer. He never took a lesson, but he read the cover off Ben Hogan's *Five Lessons of Golf* and played every chance he got.

In 1968, Calvin received another surprise. On a Sunday afternoon on a television in a golf pro shop, he watched Lee Elder as he competed with Jack Nicklaus in a playoff for the American Golf Championship. He had thought Black Americans were only caddies and waiters in pro golf. "It may take me six or seven years, but I will play on the PGA Tour," Calvin told his buddies. Their laughter drew stares from across the room.

It took Calvin almost eight years, but in the spring of 1975, after three failed attempts, the 32-year-old qualified for the PGA Tour. In 1979, Calvin won his first PGA tournament, the Greater Milwaukee Open, and from 1982 to 1986, he was the winningest player on tour. At 5-feet-10-inches tall and 150 pounds, he didn't hit the ball far, but he always hit it straight.

For ten consecutive years (1980-90) Calvin Peete led the PGA in hitting fairways with his drives earning the nickname "Mr. Accuracy" from his fellow golfers. Today, he remains the most accurate golfer ever to play on the PGA Tour.

One of the cardinal rules for a great golf swing is to keep your elbows straight through the swing. Because of the injury in his youth, Calvin could not straighten his left elbow, so he learned to compensate. Ironically, it was his odd swing that resulted in his incredible accuracy.

A golf analyst once asked Calvin, who was revered for his long hours on the practice range, "Why do you work so hard on your game?" He reflected to the hot days in the South Florida vegetable fields, then smiled and responded, "Golf ain't work."

REFERENCES

Bird, Aaron. "Calvin Peete's Self-Taught Style Still Inspires on the PGA Tour." Golf. Golf.com, December 31, 2018. https://golf.com/news/calvin-peetes-self-taught-style-still-inspires-on-the-pga-tour/.

"Calvin Peete, Golfer - Obituary." The Telegraph. Telegraph Media Group, May 1, 2015. https://www.telegraph.co.uk/news/obituaries/11577426/Calvin-Peete-golfer-obituary.html.

Posnaski, Joe. "Peete worked to achieve a miracle career." Golf Channel, April 29, 2015.

Ross, Helen. "Golf's Most Unlikely Success Story." PGATour. PGATOUR.COM, March 2, 2017. https://www.pgatour.com/long-form/2017/02/21/calvin-peete-unlikely-path.html.

Strege, John. "Calvin Peete, 1943-2015: One of Golf's Least Likely Champions." The Loop. GolfDigest, April 29, 2015. https://www.golfdigest.com/story/calvin-peete-1943-2015-one-of.

FIGHT ONE MORE ROUND

"You become a champion by fighting one more round. The man who always fights one more round is never whipped."
Jim Corbett

September 7, 1892, 9:00 p.m. – New Orleans, Louisiana: On a hot, sultry night in New Orleans more than 10,000 men, and a few women, crowded into the recently electrically illuminated Olympic Club to watch the Heavy Weight Boxing Championship. Tickets to the match ranged from $5 to $15, a price only the rich could afford. Many in attendance disagreed with the new "sissy" Queensbury rule requiring boxing gloves to be worn for the first time; real boxing involved bare knuckles and bloody noses.

There was a carnival atmosphere in the French Quarter. Newspapers across the country covered the biggest pugilistic event of the century. Two thousand miles away, beacon lights on top of the Pulitzer Building in New York City would indicate to New Yorkers which fighter won the round—red for the champion and white for the challenger.

The title fight featured legendary bare-knuckled champion John L. Sullivan, also known as "The Boston Strong Boy." The son of parents who fled the Irish potato famine, the hard-hitting, hard-drinking 34-year-old boxer embodied the spirit of the fighting Irish. During an 1887 match, Sullivan broke his left arm in the first round of the fight but fought five more rounds with his right hand before the match ended in a draw. Sullivan's handlebar mustache, womanizing, and run-ins with the law endeared him to newspaper reporters.

Sullivan had won the heavy weight-boxing crown in 1882 and successfully defended his title for ten years. He was unbeaten in his forty-fight career. In the era of last-man-standing-wins-the-bout, Sullivan knocked out challenger Jake Kilrain in the 75th round during his last championship defense. The heavy betting indicated that no one believed Sullivan could be beaten.

In the other corner was challenger James J. "Gentleman Jim" Corbett. He represented a new era in boxing. Corbett had never fought with his bare hands. Rather than learn the trade in the streets or bar rooms, he learned boxing technique in the clubs and gyms around San Francisco. The son of a preacher, Corbett had been an actor, attended college, and worked as a bank clerk before becoming a boxer. Corbett at 6-foot-1 and 185 pounds was outweighed by almost 30 pounds, but was much quicker on his feet.

During the first few rounds, fans booed the dapper collegian as he deftly dodged the punches of the champion. But they were standing in their seats when Corbett broke Sullivan's nose in round three. With blood dripping from his nose, Sullivan charged Corbett for the next several rounds like a raging bull. Corbett's ability to side-step punches and his nimble footwork frustrated Sullivan and the crowd who were there to see Sullivan thrash the challenger.

By the twentieth round, it seemed the fight might go another ten to fifteen rounds. But early in the twenty-first round, Corbett landed a hard left hook to Sullivan's jaw, and he wobbled. After two quick punches, Sullivan was on his back on the canvas. Pandemonium broke out as the trainer carried the dazed Sullivan to his corner.

After the fight, a reporter asked Corbett, "How do you become the heavy weight boxing champion of the world?" Corbett answered, "The most important thing to do is to fight one more round."

The 1892 bout would be last of John L. Sullivan's career. He retired to Boston and toured the country starring in vaudeville shows and theatrical productions. Jim Corbett boxed for ten more years with a mediocre career record of ten wins, four losses, and three draws. But Gentleman Jim would forever be remembered as the man who knocked out John L. Sullivan.

REFERENCES

"'Gentleman Jim' Corbett Knocks out John L. Sullivan, 1892." EyewitnesstoHistory.com, 2004. http://www.eyewitnesstohistory.com/corbett.htm.

"John L. Sullivan." Badass of the Week. Accessed March 31, 2022. https://www.badassoftheweek.com/sullivan.

"John L. Sullivan." Encyclopedia Britannica. Encyclopedia Britannica, inc. Accessed March 31, 2022. https://www.britannica.com/biography/John-L-Sullivan.

Klein, Christopher. "Fighting Irishman John L. Sullivan's Epic Encounters." Biography.com, March 17, 2005.

"When Nellie Bly met the Great John L (Summer 1889)." PaulBeston.com, March 6, 2017.

IT AIN'T OVER 'TIL IT'S OVER

"If you have made mistakes, even serious ones, there is always another chance. What we call failure is not falling down but staying down."
Mary Pickford

More than thirty years later, Bob Brenly still gets letters from pastors. They want him to know that they used what happened to him in September 1986 as a teaching moment in a sermon. Mike Krukow, a San Francisco Giants pitcher, would agree. After that bizarre major league baseball game, he told Brenly, "It wasn't a game, it was a sermon."

September 14, 1986 – Candlestick Park, San Francisco, California: The San Francisco Giants were hosting the Atlanta Braves on a chilly fall afternoon. Bob Brenly, the Giants catcher, started the game at third base because of an injury to Chris Brown, the regular third baseman.

In the fourth inning, Brenly booted a routine two-hop ground ball off the bat of Braves cleanup hitter Bob Horner. First error. Two batters later, with the bases loaded, Brenly bobbled another easy grounder, then picked the ball up and threw to home plate. The ball sailed fifteen feet over the catcher's head—two errors on one play.

After the third error in the inning, Giants' pitcher Mike Lacoss, a fierce competitor, walked over toward Brenly. "You might as well decide you're going to catch one sooner or later," he said sarcastically, "because there is another one coming your way." Three batters later, Brenly booted an easy ground ball for his fourth error. He threw his hands in the air as if in surrender.

Unbeknownst to Brenly, he had set a major league baseball record: four errors in one inning. A record that none ever care to break.

When the inning was finally over, an embarrassed and humiliated Brenly asked Giants Manager Roger Craig to take him out of the game. Craig growled, "It ain't over 'til it's over. Stay in the game."

With the Braves leading 4-0 after the four-error debacle, Brenly partially redeemed himself by hitting a leadoff home run in the fifth inning to make the score 4 to 1. In the top of the seventh inning, when Roger Craig came to the mound to replace Lacoss, he ranted at Craig, "You're taking me out of the (bleeping) game?" Then pointing at Brenly, he shouted, "Take him out of the (bleeping) game. It's not my fault."

In the bottom of the seventh inning with the Giants down 6 to 2, Brenly came to the plate with the bases loaded. He singled to left field driving in two runs. The

Giants trailed 6 to 4. Then with two outs in the ninth inning and the score tied 6-6, Brenly came to the plate again. On a full count, he hit a walk-off game-winning home run. Giants 7, Braves 6. Bob Brenly had balanced the ledger. His four errors allowed four unearned runs, and his two home runs and a single drove in four runs.

In 1987, Brenly made the National League All-Star team as a catcher and helped lead the Giants to a division title. He retired from baseball two seasons later. He managed the Arizona Diamondbacks for four years and in 2001 took them to their only World Series Championship.

Bob Brenly has spent most of the past fifteen years as a baseball broadcaster, first with the Chicago Cubs and today with the Arizona Diamondbacks. Each year on the anniversary of his four-error game, his broadcast buddies play a clip of his dubious distinction. According to Brenly, "The story has lived on, whether I want it to or not." He jokes, "I should have gotten 'Come Back Player of the Year' for that game."

REFERENCES

Brisbee, Grant. "It's the 30th anniversary of Bob Brenly's four-error, two-homer game." SBNation.com, September 30, 2016.

Brown, Daniel. "Giant's nuttiest game ever? Bob Brenly thinks so, even 30 years later." Bay Area News Group, September 14, 2016.

"Giant's Brenly Makes Four Errors in Inning, Then Makes Up for Them." *Los Angeles Times*, September 15, 1986.

Jenkins, Bruce. "Candlestick Memories: Brenly's 4-Error, 4-RBI Game, 1986." SFGATE. San Francisco Chronicle, December 20, 2013. https://www.sfgate.com/sports/jenkins/article/Candlestick-memories-Brenly-s-4-error-4-RBI-5080410.php.

REACHING THE OTHER SHORE

"Isn't life about determining your own finish line? This journey has always been about reaching your own other shore, no matter what it is, and that dream continues."
Diana Nyad

2010 – Miami, Florida: Diana Nyad's fire had gone out. With her sixtieth birthday on the horizon, she needed a big goal to re-fire her competitive spirit. She quietly decided to attempt the challenging Cuba to Key West swim, which had eluded her three decades before. The Florida Straights were notorious for large sharks, nasty jellyfish, and rough Gulf Stream currents which had terrified Nyad before.

When Diana Nyad was five years old, her father pointed to her name in the dictionary: Diana, a Greek goddess. He said to her, "Someday you will be a famous swimmer like Diana." By the time Nyad discovered that her Greek namesake was the moon goddess and had nothing to do with swimming, she was obsessed with swimming.

Nyad won three Florida high school state championships in the backstroke. While at Lake Forest College in Illinois, she was introduced to long-distance swimming. In 1970, she set a women's world record of four hours and twenty-two minutes while swimming in her very first ten-mile race in Lake Ontario.

In 1975, during her second attempt to swim around New York's Manhattan Island, she broke a fifty-year-old record with a time just under eight hours. By her early twenties, Nyad was becoming a star in the new sport of open water distance swimming.

In 1978, Nyad set her sights on breaking the open ocean distance record of fifty-eight miles. She decided to swim from Havana, Cuba, to Key West, a distance of 110 miles. She made it fifty miles in forty-two hours before quitting due to high waves and severe jellyfish stings. A year later, she smashed the record by swimming 102 miles from the Bahamas to Florida, arriving on to the beach on her thirtieth birthday. Afterward, Nyad declared that she would never swim again.

Over the subsequent years, Nyad earned a master's degree in literature from New York University. She worked for Fox Sports and CBS, covering Olympic and world swimming championships. She also did international travel documentaries and had a regular program on National Public Radio.

When Nyad decided to attempt the Cuba to Key West swim again, she had to start from scratch. In addition to training for another Cuba to Key West attempt, she had to raise money and recruit sponsors for her swim. She needed to cover the cost of boats and a support team, which included shark experts, oceanographers, medical advisors, and nutritionists. Nyad began her training by swimming six hours a day in a lap pool before moving to open ocean and tackling twelve to sixteen-hour swims every other day. After several 24-hour swims, she was ready.

On August 7, 2011, more than thirty-three years after her first attempt at the Cuba to Key West swim, Nyad entered the water at Havana. Strong currents and winds pushed her miles off course, and after twenty-nine hours in the water she aborted the swim. A month later, she began the third attempt. This time after 41 hours and 67 miles she stopped because of unfavorable currents. In August 2012, Nyad began her fourth attempt, but after two days of swimming, she once again stopped due to thunderstorms and jellyfish stings to her face.

Refusing to give up on her goal, on August 31, 2013, Nyad began the fifth try. This time she was protected from jellyfish by a specially designed silicone facemask, a full bodysuit, gloves, and booties. At 1:55 p.m. on Monday, September 2, 64-year-old Diana Nyad became the first person to complete the Cuba to Florida swim in 53 hours.

On her fifth attempt, the wind and currents were favorable. Those closest to Nyad joked that Mother Nature finally relented because she realized that Nyad would not be denied her goal, but would die trying.

REFERENCES

Hajek, Daniel. "From Cuba to Florida: Diana Nyad's Final Attempt at a Record-Breaking Swim." *National Public Radio*, May 31, 2015.

Nyad, Diana. "Extreme Swimming with the World's Most Dangerous Jellyfish." TED: Ideas Worth Spreading. October 2011. https://www.ted.com/talks/diana_nyad_extreme_swimming_with_the_world_s_most_dangerous_jellyfish.

Nyad, Diana. "Never, Ever Give Up." TED: Ideas Worth Spreading. December 2013. https://www.ted.com/talks/diana_nyad_never_ever_give_up.

Sloane, Matt. "Never, Ever Give Up: Diana Nyad Completes Historic Cuba to Florida Swim." CNN, September 3, 2013.

RUNNING FOR DREAMS

"Don't limit your challenges;
challenge your limits."
Jerry Dunn

2013 – Los Angeles, California: In 2013, Matthew Barnett had chest pains while playing in a church softball game and was diagnosed with a pulmonary embolism. The doctor told him, "You're going to live, but you will never run a marathon." This was fine with Barnett who had never considered the crazy idea—at least not until a few months later when an employee challenged him to run the Los Angeles Marathon to raise money for the Dream Center.

As a young boy, Matthew dreamed of a church that would remain open 24 hours a day, 365 days a year. His father, Tommy Barnett, the pastor of one of the three largest churches in America, inspired Matthew to start an inner-city ministry in Los Angeles. In September 1994, with the help of a handful of people, the nineteen-year-old started the Dream Center.

A year after his pulmonary embolism, a stubborn Matthew completed the Los Angeles Marathon to raise money and prove his doctor wrong. Although, his effort raised several hundred thousand dollars, Matthew never wanted to run 26.2 miles again. At least not until Dream Center employees suggested that he run the marathon every year to raise much-needed funds.

By 2016, Matthew had completed four marathons when a church member mentioned the World Marathon Challenge to him. The challenge involved running seven marathons on seven continents in seven days. Matthew thought it was the craziest thing he ever heard of. But when a member offered to donate $100,000 to the Dream Center, he changed his mind.

Matthew arrived in Antarctica on January 23, 2017, along with thirty-two other competitors. He survived 50 mile-per-hour winds and a minus 35-degree wind chill and completed the marathon in five hours.

His next stop was Punta Arenas, Chile. With great weather, Matthew completed the race in four hours. Then, they were off on a twelve-hour flight to Miami, Florida. Matthew's family and several church members were there to cheer him through the race, and he completed marathon number three in just over four hours.

Day four found the runners in Madrid, Spain. Midway through the race, Matthew partially tore the patella tendon in his left knee. Discouraged and disappointed, he thought about quitting the race and going home. But then he remembered the men in Alcoholics Anonymous who promised to complete the program if he completed the challenge. And he thought about the thirty-year-old single mom who agreed to finish her GED program if he finished. Matthew hobbled across the finish line in six hours.

Despite the searing pain in his knee, Matthew decided to attempt one more marathon. The race in Marrakesh, Morocco, was held on a two-mile loop lined with lampposts. Matthew ran from lamppost to lamppost and surprised himself by finishing in a little over six hours. This encouraged him enough to tackle another marathon.

Hi next stop was Dubai. Struggling in the desert heat in the early miles, Matthew was joined in the race by a man who had never run a marathon. He told Matthew that God had instructed him to help the preacher finish the race. Strengthened by the support and the encouragement, Matthew finished the race twenty minutes under the eight-hour cutoff time.

During the flight to the final marathon in Sydney, Australia, Matthew collapsed on the plane. Doctors determined he was okay, but dehydrated and exhausted. After two bags of fluids, Matthew was given the green light to run. The pastor of Hillsong Church, who had never run a marathon, and several of his church members showed up and ran the marathon with Matthew.

After sleeping only fourteen hours in a week, 42-year-old Matthew Barnett completed the final marathon of the World Marathon Challenge in 6 hours and 47 minutes. He raised $1.4 million for the Dream Center.

Today, the Dream Center occupies all six floors of the former Queen of Angels Hospital and houses more than 800 homeless veterans, addicts, alcoholics, and those down on their luck. Each month, the ministry disburses $2 million dollars of food to more than 50,000 people. Barnett's Dream Center started an international movement that has resulted in more than one hundred dream centers across America and around the world.

REFERENCES

"About." Dream Center Foundation. Accessed April 1, 2022. https://dreamcenterfoundation.org/.

Clemmons, Anna Katherine. "The Gruel and Glory of the World Marathon Challenge." *ESPN*, February 7, 2017.

Say Yes to More Things. Written and performed by Matthew Barnett. Church of the Highlands, July 5, 2017.

Van Veen, Dan. "Seven Marathons in Seven Days on Seven Continents – All for a Dream!" *PE News*, February 15, 2017.

THREE STRIKES

"I didn't see it then, but it turned out that getting fired from the Apple CEO position was the best thing that could have ever happened to me. It freed me to enter one of the most creative periods of my life."
Steve Jobs

June 16, 1995 – St. Louis, Missouri: Cardinals baseball team Manager Joe Torre was at home when he got a call from team General Manager Walt Jocketty saying he was on his way to Torre's house. Torre told his wife, Ali, "I think we're getting fired here." After five straight losing seasons and the team currently mired in a thirteen-game losing streak, the handwriting was on the wall.

With tears in his eyes, Jocketty told Torre, "Joe, we have got to make a change." Although not totally surprised, the Torres were hurt. This was the third time Torre had been fired as a big-league manager, but this firing was particularly painful because Torre had once been an All-Star catcher for the Cardinals.

Joe Torre grew up in Brooklyn, New York, and signed a contract with the Atlanta Braves after high school. In

1962 he was second in the Rookie of the Year balloting as a catcher. In a sixteen-year career with the Braves and the Cardinals, Torre made the All-Star team nine times and was the 1971 National League Most Valuable Player.

Torre got his first big league managing job in 1977 when the New York Mets hired him 45 games into the season. He managed the Mets through five straight losing seasons compiling a dismal 286-420 win-loss record before getting fired after the final game of the 1981 season.

A week later, the Atlanta Braves hired Torre. After one week on the job, General Manager John Mullen informed him, "You weren't our first choice, but let's make the most of it." Despite a winning record and leading the Braves to a National League Division title in 1982, Torre lasted only three seasons before being fired by owner Ted Turner.

After being fired from the Braves, Torre contacted several teams about a job, but none were willing to take a chance on him. His only offer was from the Cardinals to manage their AAA minor league club. At this point, Torre gave up on managing and settled for a television broadcast booth position with the Los Angeles Angels.

Torre spent six seasons covering Angel games and, although it gave him something to do, he never lost his desire to lead a team to the World Series. "I played in the big leagues for 16 years," said Torre. "But I always wanted to be in the World Series."

In 1990, Torre was given a third chance to manage when the Cardinals tabbed him to manage their big-league club. He led them to a 351-354 record through six seasons before Walt Jocketty showed up at his house in June 1995 with the bad news.

The 55-year-old Torre figured it was "three strikes and you're out," but a year later he got a call from the New York Yankees, the team he dreamed about while growing up in Brooklyn. Despite blistering criticism from the New York papers, Yankees owner George Steinbrenner hired Torre as manager even with his career record of 894 wins-1,003 losses.

That year, after 31 seasons as a player and manager, Torre finally made it to the World Series, and his Yankees beat the Braves to win the championship. He managed the Yankees for 10 seasons, winning four World Series, three of which were consecutive. Joe Torre has more post-season wins (84) than any manager in big league history, and in 2014 he was inducted into the Major League Baseball Hall of Fame.

Joe Torre's advice: "If it's a tough time right now, don't look for a reason why it's happening, just deal with it. Get through it and you'll be better for it. Move on. Tough times don't last, but tough people do."

REFERENCES

"Joe Torre Managerial Record." Baseball Reference. Accessed April 1, 2022. https://www.baseball-reference.com/managers/torrejo01.shtml.

"Joe Torre." National Baseball Hall of Fame. https://baseballhall.org/hall-of-famers/torre-joe.

"Joe Torre Safe at Home Foundation." Safe At Home, March 3, 2022. http://www.joetorre.org/.

"Joe Torre." Wikipedia. Wikimedia Foundation, February 4, 2022. https://en.wikipedia.org/wiki/Joe_Torre.

Mackay, Harvey. *We Got Fired: And It's the Best Thing That Ever Happened to Us.* New York: Ballantine Publishing, 2005. 118-125.

ADDICTIONS

"All men should strive to learn before they die, what they are running from, and to, and why."
James Thurber

February 1, 2004 – Mammoth Mountain – Mammoth Lakes, California: It was another day of crystal meth and snowboarding. Eric was addicted to both. Ignoring the ski patrol's warning that the mountain was closing because of an approaching blizzard, he planned to make one final run on a double-black diamond slope on the backside of the mountain before dark.

Eric had dressed lightly that day, expecting a high of thirty degrees. He wore only a light ski jacket, had removed the insulated liner from his ski pants, and wore cotton socks rather than water-resistant ones. He forgot to take his two-way radio with him or let anyone know where he was going; however, he didn't forget his little bag of white powder. Eric made the critical mistake of underestimating the timing and severity of the storm. He got caught in a whiteout on the backside of the mountain at 11,000 feet.

Eric LeMarque was born in 1971 and grew up in Los Angeles. He started playing hockey at age five and dreamed of playing professional hockey for his favorite team, the Boston Bruins. At Northern Michigan University he was a standout player, and he went on to play four years of pro hockey in France followed by two more years in Germany. With dual citizenship, he played on the French hockey team in the 1995 Olympics in Lillehammer, Norway.

In 2000, Eric retired from hockey at age thirty and got a sales job with Easton Sports, a large sporting goods company. But he missed the glamour of professional hockey and a year later, he quit and found two new addictions: crystal meth and snowboarding. Gaunt and hollow-eyed, he lost a lot of weight and was arrested once for possession.

By the time Eric got lost in the blizzard in February 2004, he was doing meth almost daily. He spent the first night of the storm shivering in the snow. At daylight, he started hiking, thinking he knew the direction to the lodge. He didn't. His trek in the thigh-deep snow took him in the opposite direction.

By the third day, Eric's feet were black and frozen. He knew that if he survived, he would lose them. The fourth night brought colder temperatures and another storm. Starved, frozen, exhausted, and in withdrawal,

Eric prayed for the first time in a long time. He prayed that someone would realize he was missing.

That someone, his mother, Susan, lived five hours away in Los Angeles. Eric hadn't returned her phone calls, and she instinctively knew he was in trouble. She prayed that God would keep Eric alive. Susan located the condo where Eric had been staying and notified the ski patrol. A search begun for a body. No one could have survived for five days in the sub-zero temperatures on the mountain.

By day six, Eric was too exhausted to move. He dug a snow cave and waited to die. Two days later, he heard a helicopter and turned on his almost dead, MP3 player radio. The Blackhawk picked up the weak signal on the backside of the mountain and used infrared equipment to find Eric. He had hiked seven miles in the wrong direction from the ski lodge.

Eric was close to death when he reached the hospital ICU in Los Angeles. Three days later, both his feet were amputated. He wanted to blame God, crystal meth, and the blizzard, but he knew the reason. When released from rehab, Eric went to church in a wheelchair and got on his knees. There he discovered the thing he has been searching for his whole life: the love and faith that finally satisfied the deep longings of his soul. I was on the edge of death," Eric said, "My mother's prayers saved me."

Today, Eric is married to Hope, and they have two sons. Author of three internationally best-selling books, he frequently speaks to youth hockey teams about the experience that saved his life. He works at a recovery center for those with addictions and still loves to snowboard.

REFERENCES

Becerra, Hector and Hymon, Steve. "Snowboarder Describes Days on Edge of Survival." *Los Angeles Times,* March 4, 2004.

Branson, Tim. "Eric Lemarque: A Survivor's Story." CBN.com, September 17, 2013. https://www1.cbn.com/700club/eric-lemarque-survivors-story.

Elliott, Helen. "Years after surviving Mammoth Mountain ordeal, Eric LeMarque relived it during filming of movie about it." *Los Angeles Times,* October 23, 2017.

LeMarque, Eric, with David Seay. *6 Below: Miracle on the Mountain.* Good Books Publishing, September 26, 2017.

FROM POLE TO POLE

"At every phase in your life, look at your options. Please, do not select the boring ones."
Barbara Hillary

May 16, 2017 – New School University, New York City: Barbara Hillary was honored that New School University asked her to give the address at their 81st commencement exercise. The 86-year-old had earned her bachelor's and master's degrees there. At this graduation, she received an honorary doctorate degree.

Raised by a single mother, Hillary encouraged graduates to follow a path of perseverance and determination to reach their goals. She told the audience, "We were poor, but there was no 'woe is me' in our house. My mother always told us, 'If you want something in the world, get off your butt and work for it.'"

Barbara Hillary was born in 1931 and raised in Harlem. Her father died when she was a year old, and her mother supported Hilary and an older sister by cleaning houses. While her mother cleaned, Hillary devoured books. Her favorites were about adventure—especially *Robinson Crusoe.*

After graduating from New School University with a degree in gerontology, Hillary worked as a nurse, specializing in geriatrics and training nursing home employees. Married to her career, she never had time for a husband.

In her late twenties, Hillary won a battle with breast cancer. Four decades later, at age sixty-seven, she was diagnosed with advanced lung cancer. Doctors removed half of one of her lungs and put her through a chemotherapy regimen. After recovery, Hillary retired from her 45-year career.

Hillary had always dreamed of adventure. At age seventy-two, while photographing polar bears on a dog-sledding expedition in northern Canada, she discovered that no African American woman had ever been to the North Pole. She was hooked on a new adventure.

Hillary contacted Eagles Cry Adventures, a North Pole expedition company in Atlanta, Georgia. They were skeptical about taking a woman in her seventies with a twenty-five percent reduction in her lung capacity, who had never been on skis, to the North Pole. Anticipating a risky expedition, they turned her down.

On a second phone call from Hillary, Eagles Cry suggested that they fly her directly to the North Pole so she could take pictures. She balked at that option. It took several conversations, but this woman who rarely took "no" for an answer convinced the company that she was worthy of the mission.

Hillary learned to cross country ski in Harlem, which was no small feat. The cost of the trip was $25,000—money she didn't have. With the help of GoFundMe, generous friends, and a lot of patience, Hillary eventually raised the funds. Then, she spent weeks at a local fitness center getting in shape on a treadmill.

On April 16, 2007, Hillary and two guides boarded a helicopter in Longyearbyen, Norway, that flew them to an ice station sixty miles from the North Pole. It was forty below. A week later, on April 23, after five straight ten-hour days of skiing, while pulling a fifty-pound sled, 75-year-old Barbara Hillary stood on top of the world—no worse for the wear except for frostbite on her fingers.

Four years later, on January 6, 2011, Hillary, age seventy-nine, landed in Antarctica and journeyed to the South Pole—becoming the first Black American woman to reach both poles. After returning to New York, she found a new career as a climate change activist and inspirational speaker.

Barbara Hillary never let age or poor health stop her. In 2019, despite failing health, the 88-year-old traveled to Outer Mongolia in northern China where she met with a nomadic tribe whose environment was threatened by climate change. When Hillary died in Harlem a few months later, she was planning her next adventure.

REFERENCES

"Barbara Hillary (1931 – 2019)." Barbara Hillary. Accessed April 1, 2022. https://barbarahillary.com/about/.

Barr, Meghan. "75-year-old cancer survivor skis to North Pole." *Seattle Times*, May 7, 2007.

Collins, Lauren. "True North." *The New Yorker Magazine*, March 26, 2007.

Collins, Lauren. "The Latest Dreams of Barbara Hillary, the First African-American Woman to Travel to the North Pole." *The New Yorker Magazine*, July 26, 2019.

Katz, Brigit. "Barbara Hillary, a Pioneering African-American Adventurer, Dies at 88; At 75, Hillary Became the first black woman to set foot on the North Pole." *Smithsonian Magazine*, November 27, 2019.

MARATHON OF HOPE

"I don't feel this is unfair. I'm not the only one, cancer happens all the time to people. Even if I don't finish, we need others to continue. It's got to keep going. I just wish people would realize that dreams are made possible if you try."
Terry Fox

March 4, 1977 – West Minster, British Columbia: Terry Fox's x-ray results were back, and the doctor had asked to share the news face-to-face. Rolly Fox drove his son to the appointment with orthopedic surgeon Michael Piper. Neither of them talked during the thirty-minute drive. They expected bad news.

Terry had first noticed the pain in his right knee in early November. A guard on his Simon Fraser University basketball team, he figured it was a cartilage problem and played through the pain. In February, at the end of the season, Terry visited the school infirmary for pain pills. By early March, the pain kept him awake at night.

Terry was diagnosed with Osteogenic Sarcoma, an aggressive bone cancer, which frequently starts in the knee. On March 9, the nineteen-year-old's leg was amputated six inches above the knee. The night before the surgery, Terry's high school track coach gave him a copy of *Runner's World* magazine with an article about Dick Traum, the first amputee to complete the New York City marathon. Terry told the nurses that he would do something like Traum.

A month after the surgery, Terry played golf with his dad on his new artificial leg. Chemotherapy sessions occurred every three weeks for sixteen months. Inspired by Dick Traum and moved by the sad faces and stories of those he met in chemo, Terry quietly decided to run across Canada to raise money for cancer research. He would run a marathon each day until he finished his mission.

In February 1979, Terry could only run one mile on his prosthesis. Physical therapists made changes to the leg to better withstand the impact of running. Completing a seventeen-mile race in Prince George, British Columbia, in August encouraged Terry that he could start his run in the spring. When he finally shared his ambitious goal with his mother, she was strongly opposed, but his father asked when he planned to start.

Terry gained the support of the Canadian Cancer Society, War Amputations of Canada, Ford Motor Company, and Adidas Shoes. On April 12, 1980, he dipped his stump in the Atlantic Ocean in St. John's, New Brunswick, and began his Marathon of Hope—his goal was to reach the Pacific Ocean in Vancouver, British Columbia.

Supported by his high school friend, Doug Alward, who drove a van along the route, Terry ran a marathon—twenty-six miles—each day. The response and fundraising were poor as Terry ran through the New Brunswick province, but things changed in Ontario when *Toronto Star* newspaper journalist Leslie Scrivener began a weekly column to update Terry's journey. Terry became national news.

Canadian Prime Minister Pierre Trudeau met Terry on the road in Ontario. By now, Terry had a police escort along the route. As he ran through the summer, donations, crowds, and news coverage increased. By September 1, 1980, Terry had run 3,339 miles in 143 days before he was forced to stop in Thunder Bay, Ontario; the cancer had returned in his lungs. Terry died of cancer on June 28, 1981, one month before his twenty-third birthday and nine months after being forced to quit his cause. More than $10 million was raised through Terry's Marathon of Hope.

The first Terry Fox Memorial Run was held in September 1981. A crowd estimated at 300,000 people showed up that day and donated $3.5 million for cancer research. On Sunday, September 15, 2019, the 33rd anniversary of the first run, three million people in sixty countries participated in their local Terry Fox Run. The event is the largest one-day fundraiser for cancer in the world.

The Terry Fox runs are not timed. There are no major sponsors or entry fees. Instead, the focus is on donations to cancer research and remembering Terry's indomitable spirit and his Marathon of Hope. More than $750 million has been raised to fight cancer through annual Terry Fox events all around the world.

REFERENCES

"Terry Fox Foundation." The Terry Fox Foundation, January 4, 2022. http://www.terryfox.org/.

"Terry Fox." The Canadian Encyclopedia. May 26, 2008. https://www.thecanadianencyclopedia.ca/en/article/terry-fox.

"Terry Fox." Wikipedia. Wikimedia Foundation, February 15, 2022. https://en.wikipedia.org/wiki/Terry_Fox.

Walker, Magee. "Terry Fox: The Story Behind the Canadian Running Legend." The Clymb, September 15, 2013. https://blog.theclymb.com/out-there/terry-fox-story-behind-legendary-athlete/.

GOBI THE MARATHON DOG

"The heart has its reasons which reason knows nothing about."
Blaise Pascal

June 20, 2016 – Gobi Desert – China: Dion Leonard stood at the starting line on the second day of the Six-Day 155-mile Gobi Desert Run. A scruffy little brown dog materialized at his feet. Concerned he would trip over the dog, he tried several times to shoo it away. But when the race began, the dog was still there and ran along side of him.

Several more attempts to lose the dog were unsuccessful. She ran the entire twenty-three miles through the mountains that day with Leonard, and that night she shared his sleeping bag and adopted him.

Leonard named the dog "Gobi." The little mixed breed mutt ran step for step with him all twenty-six miles of day three. Because of the rugged terrain and extreme temperatures on days four and five, race officials agreed to drive Gobi to the finish line where she waited patiently for Leonard. Gobi ran with Leonard on the final day and when he received his second-place medal in the field of 100 ultra runners, Gobi, the race mascot, got one, too.

The following day, as runners boarded buses to Urumqi, China, the departure point for home, Gobi stood staring up at Leonard with big brown eyes and a wagging tail. Leonard hesitated. "Ok, little buddy, let's go. We will figure it out later," he muttered as he picked her up. From Urumqi, he phoned his wife at their home in Edinburg, Scotland, prepared with his rationale for bringing a stray dog home. No worry. She had been following the story on Facebook and her first words were, "Are you bringing Gobi with you?"

Leonard left Gobi with race officials in Urumqi and returned to Edinburg to arrange to bring the dog back. He was surprised, but undaunted by the complicated process. World Pet Care informed Leonard that Beijing officials must approve the paperwork, then a veterinarian would check for rabies and other diseases. Then, the dog would be quarantined four months in China before she could leave the country.

The Leonards created a computer website to help with the estimated $6,500 costs of bringing Gobi home and raised the amount in less than 24 hours. Within a week, fourteen million people had seen Gobi's story on social media and newspapers around the world were asking for interviews.

Then Leonard got a call from Urumqi saying Gobi had run off and hadn't been seen for ten days. Heartbroken, he left immediately on the thirty-hour trip to China to look for his dog. He posted a $1,500 reward and spent the next week with a small group of volunteers putting up lost dog posters in the city of three million people.

The efforts seemed fruitless, and Leonard was losing hope when he received a picture on Facebook of an injured dog curled up on the side of a road. Despite a serious cut on her head and a broken right hip, Gobi squealed and jumped into Leonard's arms when she saw him.

Leonard was happy to be united with Gobi, but he no longer trusted race officials to keep his dog. He was missing his wife, out of vacation, and in a dilemma, but he felt that he needed to honor his commitment to Gobi. With the support of his wife and encouragement of his boss, Leonard took a four-month leave of absence and rented a small, shabby apartment in Beijing to care for his dog during the quarantine period.

On New Year's Eve 2016, six months after Gobi singled him out of one hundred runners, Dion Leonard and his dog boarded a flight in Beijing to return to Scotland. They arrived to find a huge crowd of family and friends gathered to celebrate their arrival.

"I don't know why Gobi chose me," Leonard told the *BBC*. "But I made a promise that I would bring her back to the UK. We battled through ups and downs, and I am glad that we got through it." In the future, Leonard plans to run the 155-mile Atamara Desert Run in Chile. He jokes, "I'm hoping a llama or alpaca doesn't follow me. I may not get away with bringing that back."

REFERENCES

Bendoris, Matt. "Finding Gobi: Story of adorable dog who was rescued by ultra-runner is the desert and brought home to Britain will be made into Hollywood movie." *The Sun Newspaper,* June 2, 2017.

Leonard, Dion. *Finding Gobi: A Little Dog with a Very Big Heart.* Nashville: Thomas Nelson Publishing, June 13, 2017.

Wang, Amy B. "Stray dog wins hearts – and new home – after following man through 155-mile ultra-marathon." *The Chicago Tribune,* August 7, 2016.

THE AGELESS DYNAMO

"I started playing slow-pitch softball at age 70, and a new life opened for me. Rise up off your butts, people, you'll feel better and live longer. It's not how old we are, but how we get old that counts."
Olga Kotelko

March 1, 2010 – Kamloops, British Columbia: When Olga Kotelko showed up at the 2010 World Masters Indoor Athletic Championship, the track officials had a dilemma. The 91-year-old was the only entrant for the 60-meter sprint in the women's 90-95 age group. With whom would she compete?

The next oldest female in the meet was 84-year-old Johnnye Vallien from California. Rather than having Olga compete in the women's 80-85-year-old category, event organizers placed her in the men's 90-95 division. Olga did not mind racing with the men, she was used to it. At her age there wasn't as much competition as there once was. She finished third, just four seconds behind 92-year-old Ugo Sansonetti of Italy who broke the world record in 11.6 seconds.

Olga was born in Saskatchewan, Canada, in 1919, the seventh of eleven children to a Ukrainian immigrant farmer. She and her siblings walked two miles every day to a one-room schoolhouse. Feeding chickens and pigs and milking cows filled the afternoons and weekends. After a failed marriage, Olga and her two young daughters moved in with her sister in Vancouver, British Columbia. There, she worked on the docks during the day and earned a teaching degree at night. She taught school until retiring at age sixty-five.

At age seventy, Olga joined a 55-and-older-coed softball league. Two years later, after a collision in the outfield, a friend suggested that she try track and field. On a track in Vancouver in 1996, five-foot-tall Olga discovered her sport. It wasn't long before the grandmother was turning heads and setting records, not only in British Columbia but around the world. She competed in the long jump, triple jump, high jump, shot put, discus, javelin, and the 100-, 200-, and 400-meter sprints. Friends talked her out of trying the pole vault due to her age and the practicality of strapping a pole to the top of her car.

In 1999 Olga set two world records and won six gold medals in the women's 80 years-and-over age category at the World Masters Track and Field Championships in Gateshead, England. At age eighty-five, she broke twenty track and field age-group world records in a single year.

In 2009 in Sydney, Australia, the ninety-year-old athlete reached a long-term goal when she finally broke the world record in the women's 100 meters in 23 seconds—a time faster than the winner in the 80-85 age group. In 2010, Olga, with twenty-three master's world records in her pocket, was honored to carry the Olympic torch at the XXI Winter Olympics in Vancouver where she lived with her daughter and son-in-law.

Olga's success intrigued gerontologists and physiologists. She agreed to become a human guinea pig at the Montreal Neurological Institute by donating blood and muscle tissue samples and submitting to brain CT scans and MRIs. To their surprise, 90-year-old Olga's cell mitochondria matched those of someone age 65. Olga's genetics were not particularly noteworthy—her father died at age seventy-four and her mother at eighty-five. She ate mostly protein, fruits, and vegetables and took a baby aspirin each day.

The masters' track and field legend died in June 2014, two months after her 95th birthday. She was the only woman in the world still competing in the long jump and high jump events in the women's over 90 categories. The ageless dynamo established thirty-seven age group world records in the 100 meters, javelin, long jump, and discus and won more than 750 gold medals in national and international competition.

REFERENCES

Editor Post. "Olga Otelko, Track & Field Notable, Dies at 95 Amid Book Fame." Times of San Diego, June 25, 2014.

Glassman, Alanna. "Ninety-Five-Year-Old Olga Otelko's Anti-Aging Secrets." Chatelaine, September 13, 2018. https://www.chatelaine.com/health/fitness/olga-kotelko-anti-aging-secrets/.

"Olgakotelko.com." Olga Kotelko – An Athlete That Inspires. Accessed April 1, 2022. http://olgakotelko.com.htmlexaminer.com/.

Stone, Ken. "Olga Otelko Dies at 95: Book Fame Followed by Years of World Records." MasterTrack.com, September 24, 2014.

MISMATCHED SHOES

"Adversity causes some men to break, others to break records."
William Ward

July 15, 1912 – Summer Olympics – Stockholm, Sweden: Someone stole 24-year-old Jim Thorpe's track shoes after he had completed three of the ten decathlon events. A frantic search for the shoes followed without success. U.S. Olympic track coach, Glen Warner, happened to find a mismatched pair in the trash and with only two hours left before the high jump event, they would have to do. America's decathlon star was not upset about the missing shoes. A veteran of adversity school, Thorpe stuffed a sock in the toe of the bigger shoe to make it fit and prepared to compete.

Born in 1887, Jim Thorpe was raised in the Native American territory of Oklahoma. His twin brother died when they were nine years old, and both his parents died a few years later. Thorpe was placed in an orphanage at age 12. Because he was half Native American, he experienced a lifetime of prejudices that came with the label "Indian."

In 1904, Thorpe moved to the Carlisle Indian Industrial School in Carlisle, Pennsylvania, the best government-run boarding school for Native Americans. Although the school only accommodated 1,000 students from age six to college age, their college athletic program competed in the Ivy League with Harvard, Yale, and Princeton.

Thorpe's athletic career began at age twenty, his third year at Carlisle, when he wandered by the track team's high jump pit and asked if he could try it. In his stiff overalls, he easily sailed over the 5'9" bar. The next day, Carlisle track coach Glen Warner summoned Thorpe to his office. "Have I done anything wrong?" Thorpe asked. "Son, you've just broken the school record in the high jump, that's all." At Carlisle, Thorpe became a multi-sport athlete starring in track, football, baseball, lacrosse, and basketball.

Primarily because of his young athletic phenom, Warner was chosen to coach the 1912 U.S. Olympic team. In Stockholm, the week before the decathlon competition, Thorpe easily won the gold medal in the pentathlon, which included swimming, horse jumping, and a three-kilometer cross country run.

On July 15, wearing his special mismatched shoes, Thorpe won the high jump. Later that day he won the

110-meter hurdles and placed third in the pole vault and javelin before crushing the field in the final event, the 1500-meter run. He established a world record time that stood for twenty-four years on his way to his second goal medal.

After the Olympics, Thorpe returned for his final year at Carlisle to lead the football team to a 12-1-1 record. He made the college All-American team by rushing for 1,900 yards while leading Carlisle to the Ivy League championship.

In 1913, upon discovering that Thorpe had played semi-pro baseball in North Carolina for $2 a game the summer before the Olympics, the International Olympic Committee revoked his amateur status and stripped him of his medals. Thorpe chose not to appeal the decision. "I won them, I know I won them," he shrugged. "I played with the heart of an amateur."

Jim Thorpe played major league baseball from 1913-22 with the National League champion New York Giants, hitting 0.327 in his final season. He also played professional football for the Canton Bulldogs for eight seasons and co-founded the National Football League in 1920. Following a successful pro sports career, Thorpe moved to Hollywood and became a character actor.

The Native American Olympic legend died of a heart attack in 1953 at age sixty-five. He is in the professional football, college football, U.S. Olympic and U.S. Track and Field Hall of Fames. The International Society of

Olympic Historians voted Thorpe the greatest athlete in history. In 1982, seventy years after his unprecedented Olympic performance, Jim Thorpe's two gold medals were reinstated and awarded to his children.

Today, in Jim Thorpe, Pennsylvania—a town named after him—stands a bronze statue of the Olympic legend in his mismatched shoes. Inscribed at the base are the words of Swedish King Gustav V who, while presenting the decathlon gold medal, remarked, "You, sir, are the greatest athlete of all time."

REFERENCES

"Biography." Jim Thorpe. Accessed March 24, 2022. http://www.cmgww.com/sports/thorpe/.

Duffley, John. "The Story of Jim Thorpe, His Trash Can Shoes and the 1912 Olympics." May 2, 2019. www.fanbuzz.com.

Jenkins, Sally. "Why are Jim Thorpe's Olympic Records Still Not Recognized?" *Smithsonian Magazine*, July 2012.

"Jim Thorpe." Biography.com. A&E Networks Television, October 14, 2020. https://www.biography.com/athlete/jim-thorpe.

Sanchez, Mary. "The True and False Stories of Jim Thorpe." *Kansas City Star*, October 25, 2015.

"Stockholm 1912 Athletics Results." Olympics.com. Olympic National Committee. Accessed March 24, 2022. https://olympics.com/en/olympic-games/stockholm-1912/results/athletics.

YOGA WITH ATTITUDE

"A journey of a thousand miles begins with a single step."
Lao Tzu

1992, Veterans Administration Clinic – Baltimore, Maryland: "Mr. Boorman, you need to face the facts," the VA doctor told him. "You will never walk again without assistance." Boorman, age thirty-two, was a former Army paratrooper who made more than 200 jumps during the Gulf War in Iraq between 1990 and 1991. As a result, he suffered from chronic knee and back pain and used a cane to get around.

For the next fifteen years, Boorman accepted the doctor's advice and resigned himself to braces and canes for mobility. He gave up on ever walking or exercising again. He got married, had three children, and worked as a special education teacher at Severna Park High School in Baltimore. Discouraged and depressed, Boorman turned to food for comfort.

By age forty-seven, Boorman saw himself as a hopeless case. His weight had ballooned from 150 to 350 pounds on his 5-foot-8-inch frame. He wore a back brace, two knee braces, and needed two canes to get around. When traveling any distance, he resorted to a wheelchair. His wife helped him get dressed and drove him to school. Boorman's preacher had to teach his kids how to ride a bike.

When a chair collapsed under his weight at school, Boorman got a wake-up call. While surfing the Internet, he came across a high-intensity yoga program. Boorman thought yoga was for sissies. Besides, yoga instructors didn't have the patience to work with a guy who couldn't stand on his own. But the program he found, developed by wrestler Diamond Dallas Page, could be done at home.

When 42-year-old Page, a two-time world wrestling champion, had been told his career was over, he came up with Yoga for Regular Guys (YRG) to help his bad back. After developing and using the program, Page resumed his wrestling career and became the world's oldest wrestling champion at age forty-three.

Although Boorman would not have been caught dead in a yoga class, he ordered a DVD. Shortly after receiving the DVD, Boorman received an email from Dallas Page asking for feedback about the program. Boorman took the opportunity to share his situation. Page called Boorman and gave him the riot act. "You are going to leave your wife a widow with three children if you don't change," Page told him.

Page decided to get involved with Boorman personally. He frequently offered encouragement through emails and phone calls. Page's biggest challenge was helping Boorman realize the situation wasn't hopeless—that he had the power to change.

Boorman began to do the yoga exercises while sitting on the side of his bed. Initially, he fell a lot, but Page's motivation kept him going when he wanted to quit. In six months, through a combination of yoga and changes in his diet, Boorman lost 100 pounds. When school started in the fall of 2007, he surprised his students at the bus stop by standing without braces and a cane when he welcomed them back.

Today, at age fifty-nine, Arthur Boorman not only can walk, but he can also run. He is back to his paratrooper weight of 150 pounds, and he is a certified yoga instructor. He is still a special education teacher at Severna Park, and he teaches yoga five days a week at a local YMCA. He also teaches yoga at a disabled veteran's program in Frederick, Maryland.

"The single biggest mistake that I ever made" Boorman says, "was letting a doctor tell me what I couldn't do. The biggest part of my journey was getting my head right. It's easy just to say I can't and retreat to fear, to lack of control, and when you do that, you are saying it is not my fault—not my responsibility. Just because you can't do it today doesn't mean that you will never be able to someday. If you never try, you will never know."

REFERENCES

Eck, Kevin. "Yoga with Attitude." *Baltimore Sun*, September 22, 2008.

Kelly, Tara. "Arthur Boorman, Disabled Veteran Walks Again After Discovering Yoga." *Huffington Post*, May 4, 2012.

Thompson, Meredith. "SPHS Teacher's Perseverance Redirects His Life." *Seven-ParkVoice.com*, January 9, 2013.

NO STOPPING HER

"God put me in the right home. 'Can't' was a four-letter word that my parents would not let me use. They taught me that everything is possible."
Jennifer Bricker

October 1, 1987 - Salem Hospital - Salem, Illinois: The baby was born without legs. Her Romanian-immigrant parents were shocked and overwhelmed. There was no money or insurance to raise a handicapped child, so they abandoned the baby in the hospital. The following day, she was placed in a foster home.

About seventy-five miles away in tiny Hardenville, Illinois, population eighty, Gerald and Sharon Bricker, hard-working, blue-collar, church-going folks, had three boys ages fourteen, twelve, and ten. After the boys, Sharon was unable to have more children. She never got the little girl she always wanted, but she never stopped praying.

Three months after the baby was born in Salem, Sharon heard from a friend that she was on an adoption list.

Sharon knew this was her baby. It didn't matter that she had no legs. Gerald and Sharon adopted the baby sight unseen. In their eyes she was perfect, and they named her Jennifer.

The Brickers chose not to dwell on the fact that their baby had no legs. They raised her like a normal child. With three older brothers, Jen became a tomboy. She was the catcher on her seven-year-old softball team and ran the bases on her hands faster than most of her teammates ran on two legs. She played basketball and volleyball, but her love was trampolines and tumbling.

In July 1996, the Brickers watched the U.S. Olympic gymnastics team win the gold medal in Atlanta. Jen was fascinated with fourteen-year-old gymnast Dominique Moceanu, the youngest American gymnast ever to win a gold medal. Jen learned that Dominique was also Romanian. Her brothers joked that Jen and Dominique looked alike, both with dark hair and big brown eyes.

Inspired by Dominique, eight-year-old Jen became obsessed with gymnastics. Her mother drove her to a gym miles away to practice. Competing against girls with legs, at age ten, Jen won fourth place in the AAU Junior Olympics in Hampton, Virginia. A year later, she won the Illinois power tumbling championship, and the U.S. Tumbling Association awarded her their inspiration award.

While watching Dominique Moceanu perform in the 1996 Olympics, Sharon Bricker suspected that the gymnast might be related to Jennifer. First, she noticed the remarkable resemblance between the two girls. Then, she checked Jen's adoption papers and the name Moceanu was on Jen's birth certificate. Further investigation revealed that Dominique Moceanu was Jen's biological sister. Concerned about complications the news might cause, Sharon chose to wait until Jen was older and interested before telling her.

Eight years after the Olympics, sixteen-year-old Jen asked her mother about her biological parents. Sharon Bricker sat her down and told her, "Your biological last name was Moceanu." Jen had sometimes wondered about the possibility, but the news was overwhelming. Her idol, whose poster was on her bedroom wall, was her biological big sister.

A few months later when Jen called her birth mother, she was blunt. "Did you give up a baby girl for adoption in 1987?" At this question, the woman burst into tears. In her broken English, she shared the circumstances. Subsequent calls from Jen to her birth mother were never answered, so Jen summoned the courage to phone Dominique Moceanu. The Olympic champion was shocked and angry with her parents for hiding the truth from her. Living in Cincinnati and expecting her first child, she needed time to process the news.

It took four years for the sisters to finally reunite, but in May 2008, Jen Bricker flew to Ohio for an emotional meeting with Dominique Moceanu. By then, Jen was living in Orlando and working for Walt Disney World. The sisters kept the information private until Dominique's book *Off Balance* was published in 2012.

Today, 27-year-old Jen Bricker lives in Los Angeles. She is one of the star performers in an acrobatic and aerial show. She tours the world, often performing in front of 20,000 people, inspiring audiences with what is possible.

REFERENCES

Bricker, Jen and Berk, Sheryl. *Everything is Possible*. Grand Rapids: Baker Books, September 6, 2016.

Bricker, Jen. "Everything is Possible." By Kelly King. *The BB&T Leadership Institute*, October 6, 2017,

Daily Mail Staff. "I Have One Chance to Prove to You that I'm Not a Crazy Person – First Letter to Olympic Star Dominique Moceanu from Legless Secret Sister Revealed." *Daily Mail*, June 10, 2012.

Peterson, Deb. "Illinois Girl Born with No Legs Doesn't Let That Stand in Her Way." *St. Louis Post-Dispatch Newspaper*, November 1, 1998.

Venema, Vibeke. "My Idol Turned Out to be my Sister." *BBC*, January 25, 2017.

DOG SLED DREAMS

"My daddy always told me to hang on...if your sled tips over, hang on, don't ever let go."
Lance Mackey

March 2001 – Fairbanks, Alaska: Lance Mackey's headaches were becoming more severe and the pea-size lump on his neck was now the size of a golf ball but taking time to see a doctor was out of the question. In 1978, his father had won the first Alaskan Iditarod Dog Sled Race when Lance was eight years old, and it had been Lance's dream ever since. Now it was his turn.

The Iditarod Race is known as the last great race on earth. The race starts in early March in Anchorage, in south central Alaska, and ends 1,150 miles away in Nome on the west coast of Alaska along the Bering Sea. Fifty dog sled teams compete over a course that covers some of the roughest and most beautiful terrain on Earth. The course features mountain ranges, frozen rivers, Arctic tundra, and miles of coastline. Throw in blizzards with temperatures as low as fifty below and long hours of darkness and you have the ultimate challenge for humans and canines.

After a grueling twelve days and eighteen hours, Lance finished a disappointing 36th place in his first Iditarod. Three days later, the mass in his neck was discovered to be a rapidly growing squamous cell carcinoma. To save his life, doctors removed neck muscle, lymph nodes, and salivary glands.

Radiation treatments damaged Lance's jawbone and resulted in the loss of ten teeth. "The doctor told me to quit dog racing," he recounts. "It made me mad. I was not going to be able to do what I had dreamed I could do. I was put on this earth to raise and race dogs, never to be rich."

After his cancer treatment, Lance ignored his doctor's warning and entered the 2002 Iditarod. Some people thought he was the toughest guy they had ever known, but most thought he was suicidal for attempting the race. Weak from radiation treatments and with a feeding tube in his stomach, he was forced to drop out near the halfway point in the race. Lance took 2003 off from racing to get healthy and to develop his dog team.

In dog sled racing, the condition and disposition of the dogs is the most important thing. Happy, healthy dogs are critical to success. Mushers devote long hours each day, seven days a week, to feed and care for their dogs. Each of the sixteen Alaskan Huskies that make up a dog sled team consumes between 5,000-10,000 calories per day.

In 2004, Lance improved his Iditarod finish place to 24th. The following year, he won the 1,000-mile-long Yukon Quest Race for the first time and finished 7th in the Iditarod. The Iditarod championship eluded him again in 2006 as he finished in 10th place.

In 2007, six years and five attempts after his first Iditarod Race, Lance Mackey finally won the event that his father helped start. His dog sled team finished in nine days, five hours, and eight minutes—covering 122 miles per day. Two weeks later he did something sled racers had long considered impossible: He won the Yukon Quest, becoming the first musher to ever win both races in a year.

In 2008 Lance won both races again. He would go on to win the Iditarod in 2009 and 2010, becoming the first racer to ever win four consecutive races. He beat the odds to become one of the greatest long-distance sled-dog drivers the sport has ever seen. "My story is a love story with my dog team," says Lance. "It is all because of my dogs. My dogs saved my life. They are my family."

REFERENCES

Black, Shelby. "Four-Time Iditarod Champion Lance Mackey Battled Throat Cancer While Competing in One of the Toughest Sports Competitions in the World." SurvivorNet, June 24, 2020. https://www.survivornet.com/articles/four-time-iditarod-champion-lance-mackey-battled-throat-cancer-while-competing-in-one-of-the-toughest-sports-competitions-in-the-world/.

Dean, Josh, Braverman, Blair, Medred, Craig, Orlinsky, Katie, and Costello, Dave. "Lance Mackey: The World's Toughest Athlete." Outside Online, June 27, 2021. https://www.outsideonline.com/outdoor-adventure/snow-sports/lance-mackey-worlds-toughest-athlete/.

Hanlon, Tegan. "For Four-time Iditarod Champ Lance Mackey, There's Only One Thing Harder than Racing: Not Racing." *Anchorage Daily News*, February 22, 2019

Iditarod, March 22, 2022. https://iditarod.com/.

"Lance Mackey." Alaska Sports Hall Of Fame, November 8, 2013. https://alaskasportshall.org/inductee/lance-mackey/.

"Lance Mackey." Wikipedia. Wikimedia Foundation, March 17, 2022. https://en.wikipedia.org/wiki/Lance_Mackey.

Yukon Quest. Accessed April 1, 2022. https://www.yukonquest.com/.

BACK ON HER FEET

"Instead of looking at our challenges and limitations as negative, we can begin to look at them as blessings, gifts that can be used to ignite our imagination and help us go further than we ever knew we could."
Amy Purdy

June 1999 – Las Vegas, Nevada: After a long day at work, nineteen-year-old Amy Purdy thought she was coming down with the flu. Less than twenty-four hours later, she was in the hospital in septic shock and on life support. The diagnosis was a rare form of bacterial meningitis with a less than five percent survival rate. Over the next two months, Amy lost her spleen, a kidney, and both her legs below the knee.

Before leaving the hospital, Amy was fitted with her new legs. The stiff, clunky legs with yellow feet were painful and cumbersome. "How am I ever going to snowboard again in these things?" Amy asked her mother with tears streaming down her face. "How am I ever going to travel around the world?" Amy spent most of the next two months in bed, ignoring the artificial legs propped against her bedroom dresser.

Growing up in the hot Nevada desert around Las Vegas, Amy dreamed of traveling the world and living somewhere it snowed. At age fifteen, she went snowboarding for the first time and a piece of her dream fell into place. Snowboarding became a consuming passion and weekends found her making the 45-minute drive to the ski resort closest to her house.

The day after graduating from high school in 1998, Amy moved to Utah—because of the snow. She entered the Utah College of Massage Therapy, and upon completing the seven-month program, she accepted a therapist position at a world-class resort, Canyon Ranch Spa in Las Vegas. Amy was living the dream, at least part of it, but she missed snowboarding on the weekends.

When Amy lost her legs, she thought her dream was over. One day as she lay in bed feeling sorry for herself, a question popped in her head. "If your life were a book, and you were the author, how would you want your story to go?" That question changed her life. It occurred to her that she was the author of her story, and she began to dream of snowboarding again. If she could just get the right legs and feet, she knew she could snowboard.

Seven months after losing her legs, Amy was back on the slopes. But snowboarding with artificial legs was awkward and discouraging. It took a year, but with a prosthetic leg designer's help, Amy finally got the right pair of legs. Those legs, and a wonderful birthday present from her father—a new kidney—enabled Amy to follow her dream.

In 2001, two years after losing her legs, Amy finished third in a snowboarding competition for adaptive athletes at Mammoth Mountain, California. Later that year, she won three medals at the U.S. Snowboarding Association event. In 2014 she won the bronze medals at the World Cup Paralympic snowboarding games in Sochi, Russia. That same year, Amy finished as runner-up in the *Dancing with the Stars* competition.

Today, at age forty, Amy Purdy is the only double-leg amputee competing at the world-class level in Paralympic snowboarding. The actress, model, *New York Times* best-selling author, and motivational speaker has been featured in Super Bowl commercials and has her own line of designer clothing. In 2005, Amy founded and continues to lead Adaptive Action Sports—a nonprofit organization that helps young disabled athletes go beyond their limits and compete in action sports.

"Losing my legs has not disabled me, but rather enabled me," Amy says. "It forced me to rely on my imagination and belief in the possibilities. Our dreams can help us force through any borders."

REFERENCES

"Amy Purdy." Team USA. Accessed April 1, 2022. https://www.teamusa.org/Athletes/PU/Amy-Purdy?pg=7.

Burford, Michelle. *On My Own Two Feet*. New York: Harper Collins Publishing, December 2012.

"On My Own Two Feet." Amy Purdy. Accessed April 1, 2022. http://www.amypurdy.com/.

Purdy, Amy. "Living Beyond Limits." TED: Ideas Worth Spreading. May 2011. https://www.ted.com/talks/amy_purdy_living_beyond_limits.

FLAT LINES AND FINISH LINES

"We can choose to endure what seems unendurable, and thereby open up the possibility of prevailing...we can embrace hope rather than despair."
Daniel James Brown

5 p.m., July 6, 2004 – Welcome, Maryland: Garth and Jo-Anne Boyle got the phone call that every parent dreads. Their only child, eighteen-year-old Brian, had been in a serious car accident while driving home from swim practice. A dump truck smashed into the driver's side of his Chevy Camaro at an intersection a few miles from their house. The fireman who called did not mention they were having difficulty extricating Brian from the car or that they didn't expect him to survive the trip to the hospital.

Two weeks before the accident, Brian graduated from McDonough High School with a 4.0 GPA. An all-state swimmer and captain of his state championship swim team, he planned to attend St. Mary's College of Maryland and be on the swim team.

Brian was life-flighted to Prince Georges Regional Hospital forty miles away from the scene of the accident. He had massive internal organ damage including an injury to his heart that required surgery to correct. Brian hung on by a thread.

During the next six weeks, doctors performed fourteen operations, did numerous blood transfusions, and resuscitated Brian eight times. By late August he remained in a coma and had developed a severe bloodstream infection. He appeared to be giving up the fight and doctors once again prepared the Boyles for the worst.

Angry and scared, Garth screamed at Brian, "Son, you're almost out of the woods. You can beat this." Jo-Anne begged Garth, "He can't hear you, please calm down." Garth continued, "He must know that he has to keep fighting. Brian, keep pushing through the pain! Please don't give up!" Garth kissed Brian on the forehead and stormed out of the room.

Despite being in a coma and presumed to be brain-dead, Brian heard his father. It was the pep talk that he needed. He slowly improved…first, a hand squeeze, a few days later a wink, and, finally, his first words. In late September, Brian was discharged from the hospital in a wheelchair, 100 pounds lighter than his previous 230.

Before the accident, Brian had three goals: go to college, be on the swim team, and complete the Ironman Triathlon. He had been fascinated with the Ironman since watching it with his dad at age six. Because of the massive damage to his chest, doctors recommended that Brian give up swimming. But a year later, with his weight back at 230, Brian was on the swim team at St. Mary's College.

Brian figured completing the triathlon would be the ultimate test of his spiritual and physical comeback. Despite his parents' concerns, and the doctor's strong objections, after a thorough medical evaluation, Brian got the green light to train for a triathlon. He completed the Steelhead Triathlon in Michigan and then contacted the Hawaii Ironman director.

After hearing his story, the race director created a spot for Brian in the October 2007 Ironman field. In the dark on October 13, with Garth and JoAnne praying at the finish line, Brian completed the Ironman Triathlon. He covered the 2.4-mile ocean swim, the 110-mile bike ride, and the 26-mile marathon in 14 hours and 42 minutes. Just 39 months after the accident, Brian Boyle was back.

In 2010, Brian graduated cum laude from St. Mary's College, ran his first 50-mile ultra-marathon, and completed his third Ironman triathlon. He is currently studying for a master's degree in health communications at Johns Hopkins University Brian Boyle is living proof that circumstances don't have to be the end of anyone's story.

REFERENCES

Boyle, Brian and Katovsky, Bill. *Iron Heart*. New York: Skyhorse Publishing, November 2011.

Mayfield, James. "An Athlete's Iron Heart." *Success Magazine,* January 2012.

Brianboyle, "Iron Heart." Iron Heart, November 6, 2018. http://www.brianboyle.wordpress.com/.

"Iron Heart Brian Boyle." Ironheart. Accessed April 1, 2022. http://www.ironheartbrianboyle.com/.

Van Allen, Jennifer. "Survival of the Fittest." *Runner's World Magazine*, April 2010.

A NEW CHAPTER

"No matter how hard it got, I always believed that the only thing worse than carrying on would be to quit."
Rosalind Savage

2003 – London, England: Rosalind Savage was divorced, overweight, and out of shape. She had spent the past eleven years working in a cubicle for a London computer company and hated her job and miserable life. One day at work, she wrote two obituaries. The first one about the conventional, ordinary life that she was living, the second about a life of adventure that she would like to live. At age thirty-six, Savage became a most unlikely adventurer.

Savage was born in Leeds, England, the daughter of two Methodist ministers. Her parents frequently moved between churches and Savage lived the life typical of a preacher's kid. As a child, she was the one chosen last when it came to neighborhood teams. Savage loved books and eating. By her teens, her big appetite and aversion to exercise had resulted in plenty of unwanted pounds on her 5-foot-4 frame.

After high school, Savage attended Cambridge University in Cambridge, England. When a crew team member mentioned that rowing workouts burned 5,000 calories a day, she was intrigued. Loving the idea of eating all she wanted without gaining weight, Savage tried out for the team. She was chosen for the number two position on the women's crew team and rowed for three years at Cambridge. After graduation, Savage continued competitive rowing on the Thames for five years before workouts got lost in the busyness of the twelve to fourteen-hour days in the corporate world.

After the obituary exercise, Savage quit her job. She sold everything she owned and used the money from her savings and divorce settlement to buy a 24-foot ocean rowboat. Her idea for a must-be-more-to-life adventure was way off the absurd chart. Savage planned to enter the 2005 Atlantic Rowing race—a rowing race across the Atlantic Ocean. The annual event, which began in 1997, was billed as the "world's toughest rowing race," without any hint of exaggeration.

Savage only had fourteen months to prepare for the race which began in the Canary Islands off the west coast of Africa and ended in Antigua, in the Caribbean Sea 3,000 miles to the west. Only about 300 boats had successfully rowed across the Atlantic—most being those with two, three, or four person crews. Savage would be the first solo woman to compete in the 26-boat race. She prepared by rowing for up to twelve hours a day on the Thames River, but rowing on the river to prepare for the Atlantic was like climbing stairs to scale Mt. Everest.

The race began on November 30, 2005. On day one, Savage's water-maker, her most important piece of equipment failed. Embarrassed, she had to radio for instructions on how to repair the equipment. Day two found her seasick and throwing up over the boat railing. During the first month, Savage developed saltwater boils on her posterior and tendinitis in her shoulders. At some point, all four oars broke, requiring splinting, and her stove failed. Savage discovered that getting out of your comfort zone is extremely uncomfortable.

During the race, Savage almost gave up on numerous occasions. The physical challenges were unimaginable, but the psychological ones were worse. She frequently threw her oars down in disgust, screamed and cried, but she realized that she alone had volunteered for the race and the only way out was to row. So, she picked up her oars and returned to rowing. On good days, she rowed for twelve hours and covered thirty miles. On bad days, the wind blew her five to seven miles in the wrong direction. She finished dead last, a full two months behind the winner and 103 days after she began, but on March 12, Savage rowed into Antigua.

Today, Roz Savage is the author of three books and numerous magazine articles. She is sought-after motivational speaker on courage, resilience, and change. Savage holds four Guinness World Records for ocean rowing, including the first woman to row solo across the Atlantic, Pacific, and Indian Oceans.

REFERENCES

"About." Roz Savage, July 4, 2017. https://www.rozsavage.com/about/.

Bradley, Ryan. "Roz Savage: Adventurer of the Year." *National Geographic*, December 6, 2010.

Prior, Matt. "Roz Savage – How Adventure Had an Impact on My Life." Medium.com, June 12, 2016.

Savage, Rosalind. *Rowing the Atlantic: Lessons Learned on the Open Ocean.* New York: Simon & Schuster, October 2010.

Savage, Roz. "Roz Savage: Why I Gave up My Job (and Husband) to Row across the Pacific." Management Today, October 14, 2021. https://www.managementtoday.co.uk/roz-savage-why-i-gave-job-and-husband-row-across-pacific/women-in-business/article/1485058.

Savage, Roz. "Why I'm Rowing Across the Pacific." TED: Ideas Worth Spreading, April 2010. https://www.ted.com/talks/roz_savage_why_i_m_rowing_across_the_pacific.

THE COMMITMENT

"Here is the world. Beautiful and terrible things will happen. Don't be afraid."
Frederick Buechner

June 24, 1992 – Seattle, Washington: It had been three days since their tragic climbing accident on Mt. Rainier. Jim wrote a letter to his best friend. He began, "Dear Mike, I will strive to take this second chance I've been given, unfurl my wings and fly with it, and not turn inward into a dark ball. I will strive to live a strong, forward-moving, vivacious life in your honor."

Jim Davidson grew up around high-altitude painting projects. His father owned a painting business in Concord, Massachusetts, which painted tall towers and big bridges—work so dangerous that few contractors would take it on. Jim's father repeatedly preached to him, "Son, don't ever let go of the safety rope. You hold on regardless. If your hands are tired, wrap the rope around your leg and hold it in your teeth. If I fall off this tower, I expect you to hit the ground right after me." Jim learned early not to quit just because a job was hard.

Jim met 23-year-old Mike Price in the fall of 1986 while they were graduate students at Colorado State University. Jim was earning a master's degree in geology and Mike in English. Mike had grown up in Colorado and was an experienced mountain climber. He taught college students to learn to climb through the Outward Bound program. Jim and Mike dreamed of climbing Mt. Everest one day.

After summiting several mountains in Colorado and South America, Jim and Mike decided to climb Mt. Rainier. They chose the more difficult Liberty Ridge route on the north side of the mountain. On the first day of summer, June 21, 1992, after three days of climbing roped together, they reached the 14,400-foot summit. Pictures were taken, and they headed back down looking forward to a shower and a steak.

As they crossed a glacier at the 1500 feet elevation, just an hour from the car, the snow suddenly collapsed under Jim, and he fell into a crevasse—a large crack in the glacier. Mike, fifty feet back and attached by a safety rope, dug in to break Jim's fall, but he too was pulled into the crevasse. They fell eighty feet and landed on a two-foot by seven-foot ledge. Mike died within minutes. Miraculously, Jim wasn't seriously hurt.

Shock, fear, guilt, and grief gripped Jim as he sat in the dark with the body of his dead friend. He blamed himself. He had no idea what to do. Instinctively he yelled for help, but he knew no one would ever hear him. He would freeze to death. Jim was a good ice climber but scaling these sheer eighty-foot ice walls would require world-class skills.

After an hour, Jim pulled himself together and started to plan his climb. He might die in a fall, but it beat freezing. He secured Mike with a rope, in hopes of pulling him out later, took his five ice hooks, and started up the wall. He had never self-belayed; he had only read about it. He fell multiple times, but the safety rope saved him each time. It took five brutal, exhausting hours, but Jim Davidson did what seemed impossible: he climbed the sheer wall of ice to get out of the crevasse.

In the years following the accident Jim married, had children, and got busy with his job as an environmental engineer. It was years before he climbed again. The memories were too painful. But eventually, he quit his engineering job and became an Outward Bound climbing instructor.

On Sunday, May 20, 2017, on his second attempt, 54-year-old Jim Davidson stood at the 29,029-foot summit of Mt. Everest and remembered that fateful first day of summer twenty-five years earlier. His had honored his commitment to Mike Price. Today, Jim travels the country sharing his story of resilience and teaching college kids to climb mountains.

REFERENCES

Austin, Charolette. "The Ledge: An Adventure Story of Friendship and Survival on Mount Rainier." AAC Publications. Accessed April 1, 2022. http://publications.americanalpineclub.org/articles/12201236500/The-Ledge-An-Adventure-Story-of-Friendship-and-Survival-on-Mount-Rainier.

Davidson, Jim. "The Ledge & The Crevasse: Climbing & Survival on Mt. Rainier." YouTube, April 21, 2011. https://www.youtube.com/watch?v=YmUC6MJrrw4.

Davidson, Jim. and Vaughn, Kevin. *The Ledge: An Inspirational Story of Friendship and Survival.* New York: Random House LLC Publishing, July 26, 2011.

Review of *The Ledge*, by Jim Davidson and Kevin Vaughn. *Denver Post,* May 3, 2016.

Scary Interesting. "Mountain Climbing Disasters | Two Men Fall Into An Ice Crevasse On Mount Rainier." YouTube, April 15, 2022. https://www.youtube.com/watch?v=1YRs-X_eg8U.

NO WHITE FLAG

"When you add purpose to the mix of pain and patience, it gives you the ability to push on. It gives you the ability to keep going when your get-up-and-go has gotten up and gone. It gives you strength to accept and face your fears and disappointments."
Tony Evans

March 2018 - Erie County Medical Center - Buffalo, New York: Jim Kelly stared at the doctor. Cancer again. The first time, it had scared him. The second time, he was even more frightened. This time—his third diagnosis with squamous cell carcinoma in his upper jaw—Kelly responded, "So it's come back? Well, it is what it is. Buffalo Bills don't quit. Let's deal with it."

In February 1960, Jim Kelly was born in tiny East Brady, Pennsylvania, about seventy miles north of Pittsburg. He dreamed of playing quarterback for Penn State University, but when they only offered him a scholarship to play linebacker, he chose the University of Miami. Kelly was a star quarterback for the Hurricanes for four years and was later selected to the school's football hall of fame.

The Buffalo Bills selected Kelly in the first round of the 1983 draft. He started at quarterback for eleven seasons from 1986 to 1996. Kelly played quarterback with the toughness of a linebacker. Despite serious neck and back surgeries, he led the Bills to four consecutive AFC championship games from 1990-93, but Kelly and the Bills infamously lost in the Super Bowl each time.

On Valentine's Day 1997, Kelly's birthday, his son Hunter was born with Krabbe's disease, a rare genetic nervous disorder. Given one to two years to live, Hunter courageously fought for his life until he died in 2005 at the age of eight.

In June 2013, Kelly figured he had a cold sore in his mouth. When it persisted, he saw the doctor who biopsied the lesion and diagnosed it as squamous cell carcinoma. The surgery to remove the cancer also required the removal of part of his upper jawbone which was replaced with a prosthetic and a set of upper dentures. Several months of chemotherapy followed.

Kelly's remission lasted less than a year. In March 2014, the cancer was back. Although he considered himself an optimist, at times the discouragement and despair overwhelmed him. The second surgery resulted in the removal of more upper jawbone and the installation of a larger prosthetic. This time there was more extensive chemotherapy, radiation, and twelve biopsies to make sure Kelly was cancer-free.

In March 2018, on Kelly's three-month checkup, the doctor discovered cancer for the third time. During a grueling twelve-hour surgery, part of the bone from Kelly's leg was used to reconstruct his jaw. He was fitted with new dentures and pronounced cancer-free in July. That same month, he was in Los Angeles to accept the 2018 ESPY Jimmy V Award for Perseverance for his toughness, fight, and resilience.

Today at age fifty-eight, NFL Hall of Fame quarterback Jim Kelly is making a difference. His annual youth football camp in Buffalo draws more than 500 young quarterbacks, his Hunter's Hope Foundation looks for cures for Krabbe disease, and his courage inspires people everywhere to not give up on their battles.

Kelly, a man of strong faith, doesn't understand why he has two plates and ten screws in his back or a plate and six screws in his neck. Nor does he know why his son died or why he's had three bouts with oral cancer. "Sometimes I wonder, Lord, why me? Kelly comments. "But I know and understand there is a greater story. These problems are just pages and chapters in that story. This life is not the end of the story. I try to focus on the bigger story, not the present outcome."

REFERENCES

Caron, Emily. "Bills Hall of Fame quarterback Jim Kelly is cancer-free, his wife Jill, shared on Instagram." *Sports Illustrated,* January 18, 2019.

D'Andrea, Christian. "Hall of Fame Quarterback Jim Kelly Is Cancer-Free Again." SBNation.com. SBNation.com, July 26, 2018. https://www.sbnation.com/2018/7/26/17616786/hall-of-fame-quarterback-jim-kelly-is-cancer-free-again.

Neumann, Thomas. "Jim Kelly talks football, life, wrestling." *ESPN Magazine,* October 14, 2010.

Rodak, Mike. "Jim Kelly to Be Honored with Jimmy v Award for Perseverance at Espys." ESPN. ESPN Internet Ventures, June 4, 2018. https://www.espn.com/nfl/story/_/id/23695970/jim-kelly-get-jimmy-v-award-cancer-fight.

Wojton, Nick. "Jim Kelly Details Cancer Struggles: 'I'm a Buffalo Bill and Buffalo Bills Never Give up.'" *USA Today. Gannett Satellite Information Network,* August 17, 2018. https://billswire.usatoday.com/2018/08/17/jim-kelly-buffalo-bills-cancer-surgery/.

NEW BEGINNINGS

"The amazing thing is that God follows us into the blackened ruins of our dreams, our misbegotten mirages, into our house of cards that has collapsed on us in some way, and he speaks, not with the chastisement we feel we deserve, but of all things, with tenderness."
Paula Rinehart

June 4, 1986 – NCAA Track and Field Championship – Indianapolis, Indiana: Kathy Ormsby from North Carolina State, the heavy favorite to win the 10,000-meter race, was in fourth place with a third of the race remaining. Suddenly, she moved to the outside of the track, ducked under a railing, and ran out of the stadium. Her coach, Rollie Geiger, was stunned and puzzled. Assuming Ormsby was injured, he left the track and followed her. When he got to the stadium exit, she was gone.

Ormsby exited the stadium, scaled a seven-foot chain-link fence, and then ran several blocks to a bridge over the White River. There a motorist saw her climb over a four-foot railing and jump off the bridge. When Coach Geiger arrived at the bridge, he saw Ormsby's body forty feet below in a grassy area near the river's edge. He climbed down the steep embankment and found her seriously injured and semi-conscious.

Kathy Ormsby was born in Rockingham, North Carolina, in 1964. In junior high school, she went out for the track team and fell in love with running. In high school, she won the state championship in the 1,600-meter run three straight years. Ormsby graduated valedictorian in her high school class of 600 and signed a track scholarship with North Carolina State University.

At N.C. State, Ormsby enrolled in pre-med with a dream to be a medical missionary. Despite being a freshman, she was one of the top runners on the team. At mid-season, Ormsby began experiencing anxiety attacks and blacking out during track meets. Geiger arranged for her to see a sports psychologist to help her relax and to try to put less pressure on herself. He had coached very few runners as gifted as Ormsby and had never worked with an athlete who pushed herself as hard.

By Ormsby's junior year in 1986, although she still experienced an occasional blackout, she was one of the top distance runners in the country. In April, at the prestigious Penn Relays at the University of Pennsylvania, she broke the NCAA 10,000-meter record with a time of 36 minutes, 32 seconds. Kathy Ormsby was the talk of the track world and honored by being selected an NCAA Track All-American.

When the ambulance arrived, Geiger helped load his star runner on to a backboard and climbed in. Ormsby was diagnosed with broken ribs, a collapsed lung, and a fractured vertebra. Two days later, doctors informed her parents and coach that she was permanently paralyzed from the waist down.

Her friends and family helped her process through the devasting injuries, and she slowly put her shattered life back together. Kathy Ormsby went on to earn a master's degree in occupational therapy from N.C. State and for the past twenty years she has worked as a therapist at the Wilmington Orthopedic Rehab Center in Wilmington, North Carolina. Today, thirty-six years after the track meet, she is an inspiration to those who know her.

The Wilmington Rehab Center always gives Kathy the challenging cases. She shares her story about a dark, ugly night in Indianapolis in 1986. She tells patients that when it seems like the end of the world, it's not. She talks about the power of forgiveness and the importance of new beginnings. She tells them there is always hope. And on Sundays, she teaches a young adult Bible study at the Myrtle Grove Baptist Church.

"I don't know why I did it," Ormsby laments. "I'll always wonder a little, but now I am at peace with it. I have asked God, my parents, and friends for forgiveness. And I have forgiven myself. I have moved on with my life."

Kathy Ormsby's story serves as a poignant reminder that no matter how bad the circumstances, there is always hope.

REFERENCES

Associated Press Staff. "Ex-Runner Finds Peace 10 Years After Bizarre Accident." *The Spokesman-Review*, June 5, 1996.

Demak, Richard. "'And Then She Just Disappeared' - Sports Illustrated Vault." SI.com. Sports Illustrated Vault | SI.com, June 16, 1986. https://vault.si.com/vault/1986/06/16/and-then-she-just-disappeared.

Heisler, Mark. "The Ormsby Ordeal: Problem is, Kathy Wasn't the First Runner to Consider Jumping." *Los Angeles Times*, June 29, 19867.

Rob, Sharon. "Runner's World: Pressure and Paralysis of Kathy Ormsby was it an Inner Torment that Led Her off Bridge." *South Florida – Sun Sentinel*, June 29, 1986.

TEAM HOYT

"If you are unwilling to risk the unusual, you will have to settle for the ordinary."
Jim Rohn

1977, Holland, Massachusetts: Dick Hoyt was exhausted, and he had two more miles to go. His legs and back ached, and his heart pounded. In his entire life, he had never run more than a mile. Yet at age thirty-seven, he was running in a five-mile race. His 15-year-old son, Rick, had convinced him to participate in a benefit run for a high school lacrosse player who had been paralyzed in an accident.

Dick's challenge was made more difficult because he was pushing Rick in a wheelchair. They finished the race next to last, but when they finally crossed the finish line, Rick said to his father, "Dad, when I'm running, it feels like I'm not handicapped." On that day, Team Hoyt was formed, and a life-transforming journey had begun.

During Rick Hoyt's birth in January 1962, the umbilical cord was wrapped around his neck resulting in oxygen deprivation to his brain. The official diagnosis was spastic quadriplegia with cerebral palsy. When Rick was nine months old, doctors suggested to the Hoyts that they institutionalize him, concluding their assessment with the awful words, "He'll never be more than a vegetable."

The Hoyts ignored the doctor's advice. They were convinced their baby had a level of intelligence because his eyes followed them around the room. They found hope at Children's Hospital in Boston where they met a doctor who encouraged them to treat Rick like any other child. Judy Hoyt spent countless hours teaching Rick the alphabet. At age eleven, he was fitted with a computer, and by pecking out words on a keyboard, he was able to communicate verbally for the first time.

Rick's first words were "Go Boston Bruins." The computer enabled Rick to go to public schools, and he graduated from Boston College in 1993 with a degree in special education. Later, he worked at Boston College helping develop communication systems for people with disabilities.

After running that first race in 1977, Dick became obsessed with competing with Rick and did so as often as possible. Team Hoyt's list of events includes 70 marathons, 94 half-marathons, 216 ten-kilometer runs, and 247 triathlons.

Team Hoyt finished the Hawaii Ironman Triathlon, one of the most grueling athletic competitions on the planet, six times. In the Ironman, Dick swam 2.2 miles while pulling Rick in a small raft connected by a bungee to Dick's vest. Upon exiting the water, Dick placed Rick's 100 pounds on a specially equipped bicycle and rode 112 miles. And following the bike portion, Dick lifted Rick into his wheelchair and ran the final 26.2-mile marathon to the finish line. Their best finish time in Hawaii was 13 hours and 43 minutes.

Team Hoyt has completed the Boston Marathon, their favorite race, 38 times. April 8, 2013 was to be Dick's last Boston, and a bronze statue honoring the Hoyts was dedicated before the race. However, they were unable to complete the marathon. They were three miles from the finish line when terrorists exploded two bombs near the finish line. Because they were stopped by officials, and unable to complete the race, they returned in 2014 to honor their commitment.

Dick and Rick Hoyt have competed in races around the world. In 1992, they biked and ran 3,735 miles across the U.S. in just 45 days. Rick was once asked if he could give his father one thing, what would it be?" He responded on his computer: "The thing I'd most like is for my dad to sit in the wheelchair and I would push him to the finish line. No question about it, my dad is the father of the century." In 2021, after pushing Rick in 1,100 races over more than four decades, Dick Hoyt died at age 80. Today, a friend pushes Rick in races.

REFERENCES

Butler, Sarah Lorge. "Boston Marathon will be Missing One of Its Heroes." *Boston Globe*, April 14, 2019.

Pfeiffer, Sacha. "One Last Marathon for Legendary Father-Son Team." *WBUR News,* April 8, 2014.

Team Hoyt. Accessed April 1, 2022. http://www.teamhoyt.com/.

"Team Hoyt." Wikipedia. Wikimedia Foundation, December 20, 2021. https://en.wikipedia.org/wiki/Team_Hoyt.

MAMA KUBWA

"It is not the mountain we conquer, but ourselves."
Sir Edmund Hillary

December 2011, Mt. Kilimanjaro Base Camp, Nalemoru, Tanzania: The porters and guides gawked and giggled. They had never seen a climber this large on Mt. Kilimanjaro. They called her Mama Kubwa, Swahili for "big woman." At 300 pounds, Kara Whitely was the biggest woman they had ever seen attempt to climb the mountain.

Each year an average of 26,000 people attempt to climb 19,343-foot Mt. Kilimanjaro, Africa's tallest peak. It takes 5 days of trail walking, almost 50 miles, to get to the summit, and only 66 percent make it to the top. The porters quietly made bets among themselves that Whitely would not be one of them.

Whitely's struggle with her weight began at age nine. After her parents divorced, she numbed her pain with trips to the pantry and refrigerator. Classmates had joked about her weight. Because of her weight, there were no invitations to her high school prom. At her high school graduation, Whitely weighed 200 pounds and had added another 100 pounds to her six-foot frame by the time she received her college diploma.

In 2004, to celebrate losing 120 pounds, Whitely and her new husband had successfully summited Mt. Kilimanjaro. In December 2009, on her second attempt, with less than two miles to go, Whitely quit. Disappointed, defeated, and unprepared she told her family that she had a stomach virus, but they knew it was the 60 pounds she had regained.

In 2011, Whitely was working as a newspaper reporter when she had the chance to go back to Kilimanjaro with a group from the Global Alliance for Africa's AIDS Orphans program. She thought successfully climbing the mountain again would make her seven-year-old daughter proud, redeem her failure from two years before, and give her a reason to lose some weight. At base camp, Whitely was keenly aware of the porter's reaction. When she tried on her two pairs of hiking pants, they wouldn't fit over her thighs. Ashamed and embarrassed, she found a seamstress in the village to combine the two pair into one.

By the second night, after ten hours of hiking, Whitely regretted her decision. Lying in her tent, exhausted, and nursing aching muscles, she could hear the porters saying her name and roaring with laughter. She knew she did not belong on the mountain. She had planned to lose 100 pounds before the climb, and she hated herself for not training and for refusing to say no to pies, cookies, candy, and chips. But then her regrets turned to anger...She would show the porters. She whispered to herself, "Never judge a girl by her blubber, there's no way I'm quitting now."

On the fourth night, Whitely's group camped at 16,000 feet, a six-mile hike from the summit. At 3 a.m. the following morning, they set out for the summit. With a mile to go, Whitely had a pounding headache, felt nauseous, and was gasping for breath. Her thighs burned with each step, and she could barely put one foot in front of other one. It was minus ten degrees and the water bottles were frozen; her mouth was dry and she badly needed water.

She could not lie to her family again. She was the last hiker in her group to reach to summit, but Whitely touched the 19,343-foot elevation at the peak a couple hours after sunrise. The other climbers and the porters were waiting for her and cheering for Whitely to finish—none of them thought she could. The porters no longer called her Mama Kubwa; they now referred to her as Unaweza, Swahili for "You can do it."

Today, Kara Whitely is a motivational speaker and American Hiking Society ambassador. She has written for *Redbook, Runner's World,* and *Weight Watchers* magazines and appeared on *Oprah* and *Good Morning America*. She is a National Binge Eating Recovery Advocate for the Eating Recovery Center and continues to do battle with her weight.

REFERENCES

"About Me." Kara Richardson Whitely - Author, Speaker and More. Accessed April 1, 2022. https://www.kararichardsonwhitely.com/about-kara.

Whitely, Kara Richardson. *Gorge – My Journey up Kilimanjaro at 300 Pounds,* Cypress: Seal Press, April 7, 2015.

Whitely, Kara Richardson. "I was the Fattest Hiker on the Mountain." *Good Housekeeping Magazine,* March 22, 2015.

FATHER OF FITNESS

"People thought I was a charlatan and a nut, but I never regretted my lifestyle change. It's why I was put on this earth to help people get healthier."
Jack LaLanne

San Francisco, California – 1951: A doctor labeled him a "quack" and advised against his weightlifting methods believing they were dangerous and could cause a heart attack. A newspaper journalist referred to him as a "charlatan" whose exercise routines could lead to sexual impotence. Another dubbed him a health nut. At five foot, six inches and 150 pounds, sporting huge biceps, a one-piece jumpsuit, and tiny ballet slippers, he certainly looked the part.

Jack LaLanne was born in 1914 in San Francisco, California, to French immigrant parents. Despite his father dying of a heart attack because of poor health habits, his mother spoiled Jack with junk food and candy. By his early teens, he was sickly, addicted to sugar and suffering from severe headaches and depression.

A neighbor suggested to Jack's mother that she take him to a lecture on the importance of good food given by nutrition pioneer Paul Bragg. When they arrived late to the presentation there were no seats available, so they started to leave. Bragg stopped the program and had the ushers place two chairs on the stage near him.

Jack took what Bragg said to heart. That night he got on his knees and asked God to give him the strength to stop eating junk food. The following week, he quit eating junk food, became a vegetarian, and persuaded his mother to let him join the YMCA. Within a month, his headaches and stomach problems went away. He never ate dessert or drank coffee or tea again. When at school, Jack took his lunch to the football field rather than the cafeteria because classmates laughed at the fruits, raw vegetables, and nuts he brought each day.

Jack bought a copy of *Gray's Anatomy* medical textbook and learned all the muscles, bones, and tendons. Soon he was preaching the benefits of regular exercise and good nutrition to anyone who would listen. In 1936, at age twenty-one, Jack opened America's first fitness gym in Oakland, California. That same year he invented the first arm and leg weight machines.

In 1951, Jack began a daily morning TV program on a San Francisco station. The media ridiculed Jack and his methods, but nothing could diminish his optimism and enthusiasm. He was an apostle for nutrition and fitness. Jack started each exercise program with "Get off your seat and on your feet." He encouraged viewers not to neglect exercise, believing it would help them grow stronger and live longer. His show was so popular with women and seniors that it went national.

Jack performed stunts to get people to accept his seemingly radical ideas about health and fitness. On his 40th birthday, he swam the length of the Golden Gate Bridge underwater with two scuba tanks. Two years later, he set the world record for pushups by doing 1,033 in 23 minutes. When he was 45, he did 1,000 jumping jacks and 1,000 pull-ups in 82 minutes.

At age sixty, Jack swam through swift San Francisco Bay currents from Alcatraz Prison to Fisherman's wharf wearing handcuffs and towing a 1,000-pound sailboat. On his 70th birthday, he swam a mile along the Pacific coast wearing handcuffs and towing 70 small rowboats—a feat that is hard to believe, if not for the pictures.

The Jack LaLanne Show ran from 1951 to 1985 and at 34 years was the longest-running television exercise program in history. Beginning in 1930, Jack never missed a workout. He awoke each morning at 4 a.m. and completed an hour of weightlifting and strength training, followed by one hour of swimming or running. He ate two meals each day: a late breakfast and early dinner.

Jack Lalanne maintained his daily routine for more than 75 years until his death in 2011 at age 96. The man who was ridiculed for years for being a crackpot inspired millions of people around the world to live healthier lives.

REFERENCES

"About." Jack Lalanne, June 7, 2016. https://jacklalanne.com/about/.

Goldman, Tom. "Jack LaLanne: Founding Father of Fitness." *National Public Radio*, January 24, 2011.

Goldstien, Richard. "Jack LaLanne, Founder of Modern Fitness Movement, Dies at 96." *New York Times,* January 23, 2011

"Jack LaLanne." Encyclopedia Britannica. Encyclopedia Britannica, inc. Accessed April 1, 2022. https://www.britannica.com/biography/Jack-LaLanne.

Luther, Claudia. "Jack LaLanne dies at 96; spiritual father of U.S. fitness movement." *Los Angeles Times*, January 23, 2011.

ALMOST 100 YEARS LATER

"Often it is not the size of the dog in the fight, but the size of the fight in the dog."
Archie Griffin

January 1, 1926 – Rose Bowl – Pasadena, California: It was one of the most significant college football games ever played. The Rose Bowl, which at the time was the country's only bowl game, served as the de facto national championship game. The gridiron contest pitted teams from the East and West Coasts. A team from the deep South had never gotten an invitation to the Tournament of Roses.

The fearsome Washington Huskies, 10-0-1 represented the Pacific Coast Conference, but getting an opponent proved more difficult. Eastern champion, 8-0 Dartmouth turned down the invitation, as did Princeton, Colgate, and Yale. Concerned about the size and speed of the Huskies, the Tulane Green Wave did, too.

Coach Wallace Wade's University of Alabama squad, the unofficial Southern champion, graciously accepted the challenge. They were 9-0, having given up only one touchdown all season. In two seasons in Tuscaloosa, Wade's team had outscored opponents 516-74 with eight shutouts along the way.

Ten days before the game, the Tide team, twenty players strong, left Tuscaloosa on the train for the 2,000-mile, three-day trip to the West Coast. When the train occasionally stopped to take on fuel, Wade practiced his team. Plenty of wind sprints were the order of the day. The Alabama team arrived in Pasadena a week before the game to allow ample time for practices. Wade knew what was at stake. Washington's team showed up on New Year's Day.

An estimated record Rose Bowl crowd of 45,000 filled the 53,000-seat stadium, the largest in the country since its construction three years prior. In Alabama, theaters were set up with a special news wire so fans could follow the play-by-play.

College football coaching legend Glen "Pop" Warner said that Washington was just too big for the small Bama boys. Entertainer Will Rogers, when asked for his prediction, laughed and called the Alabama team the Tusca-losers.

Alabama featured two of the best players in the South: All-American quarterback Allison "Pooley" Hubert and running back Johnny Mack Brown, whom newspapers had dubbed "the Dothan antelope." After later being featured on a Wheaties cereal box in 1927, the handsome Brown would enjoy a long and successful career a few miles away in Hollywood.

Early in the game, Washington unleashed their lead dog, George "Wildcat" Wilson who was equally adept at passing, running, and kicking. By himself, Wilson stopped the Tide offense with tackles, sacks, and interceptions. Then Wilson, an outstanding running back, made all but one carry on an 85-yard drive to put the Huskies up 6-0. In the second quarter, after a 36-yard run, Wilson threw a 20-yard touchdown pass and Washington took a 12-0 halftime lead over the out-manned Southerners.

Hubert challenged his teammates, "What the hell is going on here?" The team waited in the locker room, anticipating a fiery halftime talk from Wade, but he simply stuck his head in the locker room, and in a low voice said, "They told me boys from the South would fight." A fire was lit.

On the Tide's first possession, Hubert ran 26 yards to the Washington 12. Four more carries by Hubert gave the Tide their first score, 12-7. After stopping Washington on the next possession, halfback Grant Gillis threw a 61-yard touchdown pass to Johnny Mack Brown. 14-12. The Huskies next drive ended at their own 30 after a fumble and a Hubert to Brown pass made it 20-12. Three touchdowns in seven minutes.

Washington would manage a fourth quarter score, but two Tide interceptions sealed the 20-19 victory giving Alabama its first national championship and forever placing Southern football on the map. Wade's Crimson Tide was the talk of the nation.

Newspaper sports headlines shocked the country and had Southerners celebrating in the streets. On the return trip, the train made a stop at every small town as excited crowds and marching bands welcomed the Tide.

Almost 100 years after the game that changed Southern football, the fire lit in the Rose Bowl still burns bright. And the Alabama fight song still commemorates the monumental 1925 Rose Bowl win, "For Bama's pluck and grit have writ her name in crimson flame…Remember the Rose Bowl we'll win then."

REFERENCES

Miller, Ted. "How a Win over Washington Gave Rise to Alabama and Football in the South." ESPN. ESPN Internet Ventures, December 23, 2016. https://www.espn.com/college-football/story/_/id/18325546.

"Rose Bowl of 1926." Encyclopedia of Alabama. Accessed April 1, 2022. http://www.encyclopediaofalabama.org/article/h-2033.

Stephenson, Creg. "Remembering Alabama's Rose Bowl Win over Washington." AL.com, December 28, 2016. https://www.al.com/sports/2016/12/remember_the_rose_bowl_1926_wi.html.

Tracy, Marc. "Alabama Win in 1926 Rose Bowl Put Southern Stamp on College Football." *New York Times*, December 27, 2016.

RUN, JUSTIN, RUN!

"Don't let people who question you get in your way. It's not about the legs. It's about the heart and mind. The journey is darn sure not over."
Justin Gallegos

Wednesday, October 8, 2018 – Oregon University – Eugene, Oregon: Justin was exhausted, too tired to notice the cameras. He had just finished a grueling three-mile cross-country race. As he cooled down with his fellow University of Oregon cross- country club team members, John Douglass, the Nike Insight Director, approached him.

Addressing the small group gathered near the finish line Douglass said, "Today, I am here on behalf of Nike to present Justin with a three-year contract to be an official Nike athlete." Hearing these words, Justin collapsed to his knees in tears. It was a moment he could not have dreamed of and a moment he would never forget. Nike has paid hundreds of professional athletes to wear its brand since they introduced their "Just Do It" slogan in

1988, but never had they chosen an athlete with cerebral palsy.

Justin was born with cerebral palsy, a neurological disorder that affects movement, motor skills, and muscle tone. Instead of making excuses for his disability, his parents treated him just like the other children. He used a walker until elementary school and transitioned to knee braces for several years before being able to walk on his own.

Growing up in Santa Clarita, California, Justin loved sports, particularly football, but could not participate, so his father suggested he try out for his high school's cross-country team. Hart High School track coach Darren James welcomed the freshman.

Justin fell often. Skinned knees and elbows were the order of the day. So was finishing last in races. Justin's awkward running style with his feet turned inward and his heels splayed to the side drew stares and snickers, but Justin did not quit. He was having fun.

Although he often finished last, by his senior year Justin had reduced his mile time from eight minutes, thirty seconds to seven minutes and reduced his three-mile cross-country time by five minutes. After high school, he accepted an invitation to join the University of Oregon running club team. Across town, Nike CEO Phil Knight heard of Justin's story and arranged to meet Justin at Nike headquarters.

Nike asked Justin to work with them to design a running shoe for his unique running gait.

In July 2017, Nike introduced the Air Zoom Pegasus 35 FlyEase to the market. The shoe features additional padding in the toe box and more stability in the heel for runners like Justin. Rather than laces, it has a zippered heel for easy on and off.

Justin was named one of *Runner's World* Magazine's 2017 Heroes of Running. In April 2018, he ran the Eugene, Oregon, half marathon, finishing in two hours and three minutes, just three minutes over his goal. "No amount of bloody knees and worn-down shoes can compare to crossing the finish line," shouted Justin.

John Douglass coordinated the presentation of the contract to Justin to coincide with the World Cerebral Palsy Day. It is a day established to recognize Justin and the 17 million people in the world who struggle with the condition. Douglass told Justin's teammates and friends that it was Justin's spirit that inspired Nike to offer him a running contract. Justin told the small crowd, "Growing up with a disability, the thought of becoming a professional athlete is like climbing Mt. Everest."

Nike has paid Bo Jackson, Tiger Woods, and Michael Jordan, among many other professional athletes to wear their brand, to promote winning. When twenty-year-old Justin Gallegos dons their gear, it's about overcoming, persevering, and not quitting.

REFERENCES

Gretschel, Johanna. "Justin Gallegos Still in Shock from his Surprise Nike Contract." *Runner's World*, October 15, 2018.

"Justin Gallegos Runs with Nike FlyEase Technology." Nike News, May 1, 2018. https://news.nike.com/news/justin-gallegos-flyease-technology.

Shilton, A. C. "The Rock-steady Motivator: Justin Gallegos." *Runner's World*, January 23, 2017.

Williams, Doug. "Overcoming Cerebral Palsy makes Justin Gallegos an Inspiration to Fellow Runners." *ESPN*, November 11, 2015.

@zoommagic. "I'm at a loss for words!" October 8, 2018. https://www.instagram.com/p/BoruyLoA-_e/.

THE LAST AMERICAN BASEBALL GLOVE

"Perseverance is stubbornness with a purpose."
Josh Shipp

2019 – Nacona, Texas: The sign on U.S. Highway 82 reads "Welcome to Nacona; Leather Goods Center of the Southwest." With a population of 3,000, the two-stop-light town, located about 100 miles northwest of Dallas, was once home to a many boot and belt companies dating back to the cattle drives 150 years ago. Most of the leather manufacturers are gone now. In the 1960s, they moved to places like China, Vietnam, or the Philippines.

One company did not get the memo. At 208 Walnut Street sits a 60,000 square foot brick building that stands as a monument to perseverance and a stubborn refusal to follow the herd. The Nokona Athletic Goods Company was founded in 1927 to make wallets and purses. Two years later, America's greatest depression almost killed the demand for billfolds.

Facing bankruptcy in 1934, and desperate for something that would sell, Robert Storey, a former Rice University baseball player came up with the idea to make baseball gloves. At that time, most players did not use baseball gloves—they played the game barehanded—but it was an idea whose time had come and an idea that saved Nokona.

During World War II, the company was chosen as the single supplier for baseball gloves to the U.S. military and the company prospered. The 1950s were the peak years for Nocona, and sales approached 250,000 gloves annually.

In the 1960s, with the arrival of cheap imported baseball gloves from Asia, the company almost went out of business again. Nokona refused to import cheap gloves, or make them offshore, but staked their future on the bet that Americans were willing to pay more for a high-quality item with "The American Glove" stitched into every pocket.

In addition to cowhide, Nokona began using buffalo and kangaroo hides, creating a soft but durable glove, and differentiating the company as a maker of handmade, high-quality, high-dollar gloves. They also added softball gloves to the line and were able to stabilize annual production at roughly 50,000 gloves.

On July 18, 2006, the glove factory—Nocona's main factory—burned to the ground. Company President Rob Storey, grandson of Robert Storey, announced immediately to the eighty employees that no one would be laid off and no one would miss a paycheck. He bought tickets for all employees to attend a Texas Ranger baseball game to boost morale.

The company quickly found an abandoned boot factory to use as a temporary location, salvaged a couple of pieces of equipment from the fire, and produced its first glove fifty days after the fire. By January, Nokona was back to its pre-fire production level of 200 gloves a day while the building was being rebuilt on Walnut Street.

In 2010, the company was sold to Cutter's Gloves, a Phoenix, Arizona, company who renamed Nokona "American Original Ballglove Company," but maintained the Nokona Made-in-America tradition. Robby Storey, great grandson of the glove founder, manages the day-to-day operation of the plant. As plant manager he is often asked, "Why not move offshore like the rest? He replies, "Because I am crazy. This is all I know how to do."

Today, more than ninety years after it began, the thirty-five employees in the brick building on Walnut Street make about 40,000 Nokona gloves annually in a U.S. market where six million gloves are sold. Visitors can tour the factory and a museum of the history of baseball gloves for $5. Fifty years after competitors moved overseas to maximize profits, Nokona hangs on to the American dream in north central Texas.

REFERENCES

Case, Brendan. "Nokona Glove." *The Dallas Morning News*, October 2010.

Gwynne, S. C. "Glove Story." *Texas Monthly*, March 2007.

Mayeda, Andrew. "Made in America: Nation's last baseball-glove maker refuses to die in Texas." *The Star-Telegram*, August 20, 2017.

McLeod, Gerald. "Daytrips." *Austin Chronicle*, February 22, 2002.

"Our Story." Nokona Ballgloves, August 18, 2020. https://nokona.com/our-story/.

THE FIRING OF A COACH

"Winners are not those who never fail, but those who never quit."
Edwin Louis Cole

Valentine's Day 1996 – Cleveland, Ohio: Cleveland Browns Head Coach Bill Belichick got a phone call from team owner Art Modell. Modell was to the point. "We have decided to go another direction. You and your staff are fired." The following day the Akron, Ohio, *Beacon Journal* sports page read, "Bill Belichick's Five-Year Reign of Error is Over."

Five years earlier, Belichick had finally gotten his chance to be a head coach in the National Football League after sixteen years as an assistant. After five seasons, however, his record of 37 wins and 45 losses resulted in Modell's call. The firing, particularly getting fired on the phone, was a bitter disappointment for 44-year-old Belichick. He figured he had blown his opportunity to ever coach in the NFL.

Belichick was raised in Annapolis, Maryland. His father, Steve, was a longtime assistant football coach at the U.S. Naval Academy. By age seven, he had developed a love of coaching from following his dad around the practice field. After graduating from Annapolis High School in 1970, Belichick attended Wesleyan University in Middletown, Connecticut, earning a B.S. in Economics in 1975.

Anxious to coach, Belichick took a $25-a-week job as an assistant in the front office of the Baltimore Colts. In 1977, he joined the Detroit Lions as assistant special teams' coach. Two years later he moved to the Denver Broncos for one season in the same capacity. The following year, the coaching trail took Belichick to the New York Giants. During an eleven-year tenure there, he held several defensive coaching positions before being promoted to defensive coordinator in 1985.

In 1991, when Belichick became the Browns head coach, he made plenty of mistakes. Players disliked him and complained about practices being too hard and meetings too long. His gruff demeanor with the media created problems for him, and Belichick traded popular quarterback Bernie Kosar which caused fans to hate him.

After being fired from the Browns, Belichick was hired by the New England Patriots as defensive backs coach. After a year, he followed Patriots' Head Coach Bill Parcels to the New York Jets.

Belichick had been with the Jets for three seasons when, in early 2000, New England Patriots owner Robert Kraft fired Pete Carroll, and despite strong criticism from the press and fans, offered Belichick a second opportunity to be a head coach. Despite a first-year record of five wins and eleven losses, Kraft promoted Belichick to general manager as well as head coach. That same year, Belichick drafted a little-known college quarterback from Michigan named Tom Brady in the sixth round.

Belichick's mistakes at Cleveland prepared him for success at New England. In 2001, after an early season injury to starting quarterback Drew Bledsoe, young QB Tom Brady led the Patriots to a Super Bowl win over the heavily favored St. Louis Rams. Two years later, the Patriots won another Super Bowl by beating the Carolina Panthers. In 2004, Belichick became the only coach in NFL history to win three Super Bowls in four years when his Patriots beat the Philadelphia Eagles.

Bill Belichick has been NFL Coach of the Year three times. Eighteen years after Robert Kraft gave him a second chance as a head coach, 70-year-old Belichick is still at the helm. Widely recognized as the greatest coach in NFL history, he is the only NFL coach to ever win five Super Bowls.

On those painful days of doubt and discouragement following his 1996 Valentine's Day firing, Bill Belichick could not have imagined what the next twenty-five years would hold for him. And the Cleveland Browns can only dream of what might have been. Some people rebound from a firing because they are destined to, but most people rebound because they are determined to.

REFERENCES

Altman, Bryan. "Cleveland, 20 Years Ago Today, Bill Belichick Fired by Browns." *CBS,* February 15, 2016.

Associated Press. "Bill Belichick Not Going to Baltimore." *Los Angeles Times,* February 15, 1996.

Halberstam, David. *The Education of a Coach,* New York: Hyperion Publishing, November 1, 2005.

King, Peter. "Super Bowl 51: Patriots Take Fifth in Epic Comeback." *Sports Illustrated,* February 6, 2017.

DRAG RACING'S FIRST LADY

"The value of persistence is the fact that few people have any, and you'll be at the finish line when everyone else has quit in the middle of the race."
Shirley Muldowney

1955 – Schenectady, New York: Shirley was sneaking out of the house to watch her boyfriend Jack Muldowney drag race by her mid-teens. At age sixteen, when she dropped out of high school to marry Jack, her teacher told her, "You know, Shirley, you're not going to make your living riding around in fast cars."

Shirley Muldowney's father was a cab driver and former boxer who passed his toughness and spirit to his daughter. Shirley didn't heed her teacher's advice. At age eighteen, she entered her first-quarter mile drag race at Fonda Speedway in Fultonville, New York, driving a 1958 350 horsepower Chevy. Shirley did not win, but she was hooked.

Although Shirley won several trophies, the male-dominated world of drag racing did not welcome her nor take her seriously. The National Hot Rod Association (NHRA) tried to stop her from getting a license. It took five years and the services of an attorney before Shirley was granted a license.

Shirley's battle for acceptance was just beginning. Drivers, support crews, and sponsors alike thought her place should be cooking post-race meals for them rather than driving a hot racecar. She got the mechanics that nobody wanted because it was degrading to work for a female. And it didn't help matters that Shirley painted her race cars hot pink.

It was only when the drag racing community finally recognized that Shirley wasn't going to be denied her dream that they accepted her. In 1971, she won the International Hot Rod Association Southern National race, and then there was no stopping her.

Later that year, Shirley made the national finals in the newly created Funny Car Division. However, driving the unusual fiberglass car, which burned nitro methane fuel, was dangerous due to fire risk. In 1973, after receiving severe burns when her car exploded, Shirley retired from funny car racing and moved up to the faster but safer Top Fuel dragsters.

In June 1975, Shirley made the Top Fuel dragster finals and broke the six-second barrier for a quarter mile for the first time, posting a time of 5.98 seconds going 244 miles per hour. The following year, she took the grand prize in the NHRA Top Fuel Championship and was named Top Fuel Driver of the Year—the pinnacle in a male-dominated sport. Shirley went on to win the World Top Fuel Championships in 1977, 1980, and 1982, becoming the first driver to ever win three world championships.

In 1984, Shirley was almost killed in a Montreal race when a front tire blew, and she crashed at more than 250 miles per hour. Both legs, both hands, and her pelvis were crushed. After eighteen months of rehab, Shirley made a racing comeback in the 1986 season. In 1989, she won another National Hot Rod Association title, breaking the five-second barrier for the first time with a quarter-mile time of 284 miles per hour.

In 2003, after more than forty years of racing and eighteen NHRA national titles, 63-year-old Shirley Muldowney retired. She completed her final quarter mile at 317 miles per hour. The crowd cheered as "The First Lady of Drag Racing" deployed her pink parachute and drove slowly past the grandstands for the last time. In 2004, she was inducted into the International Motor Sports Hall of Fame.

Today, the queen of drag racing lives in Huntersville, North Carolina, and is a frequent Grand Marshall at NHRA. Her Shirley's Kids charity provides support to kids with medical or financial hardships due to family tragedy. Reflecting on her career, Shirley says, "I could have quit, and nobody would have blamed me. But I didn't quit because it was my dream. I loved driving the car, the excitement of 4,000 horsepower and careening down a quarter-mile track at 300 miles per hour."

REFERENCES

Andrews, Andy. *Storms of Perfection—In Their Own Words*. Lightning Crown Publishers, 1991. See chap. 5 "Shirley Muldowney – Drag Racer."

Burgess, Phil, and NHRA National Dragster Editor. "Rethinking the Top 50 Racers List." NHRA. December 5, 2017. https://www.nhra.com/news/2017/remaking-top-50-racers-list.

Esterbrook, John. "Racing Pioneer Muldowney Retires." *CBS News*, November 10, 2003.

"Mul Downey Racing." muldowneyracing. Accessed April 1, 2022. http://www.muldowney.com/.

"Shirley Muldowney." Biography.com. Accessed April 1, 2022. https://biography.yourdictionary.com/shirley-muldowney.

A DISCOURAGING SEASON

"Failure is not fatal, but failure to change might be."
John Wooden

1933 – Dayton High School – Dayton, Kentucky: The sports editor of the Dayton High School yearbook was critical of the first-year basketball coach. "A discouraging season," the annual said of the Green Devils' six-win, eleven-loss season. In his first job out of college, the small high school's 23-year-old, newly married English teacher and basketball coach was discouraged.

John Wooden talked with his wife about quitting his coaching job and moving back to their home state of Indiana, but she encouraged him to try it one more year. In his second and final year as Dayton's basketball coach, his Green Devils made a better showing with a record of fifteen and three.

Wooden grew up on a farm in Centerton, Indiana. After the chores were done, he learned to play basketball by shooting hoops in the barn with his three brothers. In 1927, Wooden led Martinsville High School to the state basketball championship and became an All-American selection at guard at Purdue University for three straight years. In 1932, Wooden led Purdue to the National Championship.

After graduating with honors in English, Wooden turned down an opportunity to play professional basketball, married his sweetheart Nell Riley, and moved to Dayton, Kentucky, to be a high school teacher and coach.

After his second year at Dayton High, Wooden returned to Indiana to teach English and coach basketball at South Bend Central High School. In nine years at South Bend, his teams enjoyed great success, winning 218 games and losing only 42. In 1943, during World War II, Wooden joined the United States Navy and served as a physical education instructor.

After his Navy discharge, Wooden became the head basketball coach at Indiana State Teachers College. He was there for two years and won conference championships both seasons. In 1948, he accepted the job of head basketball coach at UCLA. It was not a popular coaching stop; the Bruins were the worst team in the Pacific Coast Conference and lacked an on-campus basketball facility. The basketball team shared a practice facility with other sports. In Wooden's first season, he won 22 of 29 games and in his first eight seasons UCLA won three conference championships.

After fifteen seasons at UCLA, Wooden's 1964 team went 30-0 and won their first National Championship. Over the course of the next eleven seasons, the Bruins won nine NCAA Championships including an unprecedented seven in a row. In twenty-seven seasons at UCLA, Wooden won nineteen conference championships and ten National Championships. His 88-game win streak and four 30-0 seasons remain NCAA milestones.

John Wooden was inducted into the College Basketball Hall of Fame as a player in 1961 and as a coach in 1973, becoming the first person to achieve both honors. In 1975, he retired one week after winning his tenth National Championship. In 1999, ESPN network selected John Wooden the NCAA Coach of the Century. He is perhaps the greatest coach, in any sport, to ever walk a sideline.

Regarding his coaching career, Wooden reflects, "I would have been satisfied just coaching in high school. I turned down several colleges when I was teaching in South Bend before I entered the Navy. I honestly believe that if I hadn't enlisted, I would never have left high school coaching."

John Wooden often referred to that first year of coaching at Dayton High School, his only losing team, as the most important season of his epic career. He spoke at high school sports banquets on many occasions and always told audiences, "I learned what not to do."

The students publishing the 1933 Dayton yearbook in Campbell County, Kentucky, could never have imagined that the basketball season they were covering would become legendary coach John Wooden's only losing season.

REFERENCES

Dwyre, Bill and Wharton, David. "John Wooden dies at 99; UCLA basketball coach won 10 national titles." *Los Angeles Times,* June 5, 2010.

"John Wooden." Biography.com. A&E Networks Television, October 27, 2021. https://www.biography.com/athlete/john-wooden.

Waitley, Denis. *The New Dynamics of Winning*. Wheeling: Nightingale-Conant Corporation, 1993, p. 161-164.

SURVIVAL IN THE ANDES

"You will never know what you are capable of until quitting is no longer a way out."
Edmond Mbiaka

October 16, 1972 – Andes Mountains, Chile: Nando Parrado woke to a nightmarish scene. The 23-year-old lay on the floor of an airplane looking up at the light streaming through the small windows in the cabin. Most of the seats were missing, electrical wiring dangled from the ceiling, and it was bitterly cold. He heard a mumbled voice say the plane had crashed in the mountains. His nightmare was just beginning.

On October 13, Uruguayan Army charter flight 514 left Montevideo, Uruguay, bound for Santiago, Chile. On board was the Old Christian Rugby team and some family members headed to an exhibition match. Parrado was the team captain. During a snowstorm, the plane had crashed into a high mountain valley located at 12,000 feet. Seventeen of the forty-five people on board, including Parrado's mother and sister, were killed in the crash.

The survivors, mostly eighteen to twenty-year-old men, were dressed in summer clothing and unprepared for the bitter cold. They found a few chocolate bars and candy in suitcases and hoped they would soon be rescued. But after a week, a transistor radio revealed the devastating news: the search for the missing plane had been canceled. Nobody could still be alive in the frigid Andes Mountains.

A week later, an avalanche buried the plane's fuselage, killing nine more of the group. After digging out, the remaining nineteen survivors sat shivering and crying, wishing the avalanche had taken them as well. During the next month, three more survivors gave up and succumbed to the miserable conditions.

As a child, Parrado's favorite story had been the one his father would tell about when he competed in a strenuous rowing event as a youth. Although exhausted, he had vowed not to quit but to struggle a little longer during the match. This story became a lifeline for Parrado, motivating him to not give up.

On four occasions in late November, Parrado and three other survivors tried to walk out of the high mountain valley. Each time either a blizzard or the height of the mountain peaks caused them to turn back. On December 12, two months after the crash, Parrado and teammate Robert Canessa made another attempt.

Rather than sit around waiting for death, if they had to die, they were determined to die trying to get out. Ten days after leaving the crash site, they stumbled into the camp of two ranchers grazing their cows on the high prairie near Los Maitenes, Chile. With makeshift snowshoes fashioned from seat cushions, they had walked seventy miles through deep snow and scaled a 17,000-foot mountain peak. The ranchers summoned police authorities.

When the Santiago Rescue Service asked Parrado to show them where he thought the plane had gone down on the map, they thought that he was confused. They questioned, "You are sure? It's impossible that you could have crossed the Sosneado Mountain. It is one of the most rugged peaks in the Andes. Surely you came another route." Parrado was sure. No one had told him it was impossible.

On December 22, Parrado guided two helicopters to the crash site to rescue the remaining fourteen survivors off the mountain. The rescue team was shocked to discover a gruesome scene at the wreckage. In desperation, the survivors had consumed the flesh of their dead comrades. In the weeks following the rescue, the media excoriated them for their decision.

Parrado, who spoke up for himself and his teammates responded to the criticism, "It was like a man on top of a burning building. We were forced to make decisions that men should never have to make. It is easy to say what you would do at sea level. What would you have done in the bitter cold at 17,000 feet?"

Today, 72-year-old Nando Parrado lives with his wife Veronique in Montevideo. They have two daughters. He is president of MRC, a company that produces some of the top television shows in Uruguay. He still tells the story of his survival in the Andes to audiences around the world.

REFERENCES

"About." Parrado.com. Accessed April 1, 2022. http://parrado.com/about/.

Parrado, Nando. *Miracle in the Andes; 72 Days on the Mountain and My Long Trek Home.* Portland: Broadway Books, May 9, 2006.

Shelden, Michael. "What could we eat but our dead friends?" *The Telegraph*, May 25, 2006.

THE FAN IN SECTION 724

"Nothing reduces the odds against you like ignoring them."
Robert Brault

Spring 1976 – Philadelphia, Pennsylvania: When UCLA football coach Dick Vermeil was hired as Philadelphia Eagles head coach, he inherited a team with nine straight losing seasons. Desperate for talent, Vermeil held an open tryout camp for all-comers. More than 600 primarily ex-high school jocks showed up, including Vince Papale, an enthusiastic thirty-year-old high school teacher, part-time bartender, and Eagle season ticket holder in Section 724.

Papale grew up in Glenolden, a blue-collar Philadelphia neighborhood. His father, a sheet metal worker in a steel mill, shared his love for the Philadelphia Eagles with his young son. Growing up, Papale was always the smallest but fastest kid in school. Five-foot-six-inch, 145-pound Papale finished fifth in the state pole vault as a high school senior.

On a track scholarship, Papale attended St. Joseph's College in Philadelphia and competed in the long jump, triple jump, 400-meter hurdles, and pole vault. After earning a business degree, he returned to his old high school as a teacher and junior high track coach. While playing in a Philadelphia touch football league sponsored by local pubs, he led the league in receiving and made the all-star team. Papale's success led him to a semi-pro club which played on Saturday nights at high school football fields and paid players $50 and a six-pack of beer each game.

Two years before Coach Vermeil arrived in Philadelphia, the World Football League, a start-up professional league, formed. To the amazement of his buddies, Papale made the team as a wide receiver. He caught a dozen passes before the league folded halfway through the 1975 season. He made $16,000 from playing, about $4,000 more than his teaching job.

When Dick Vermeil held his tryout camp, the now 6-foot-2, 195-pound Papale decided to give it a shot after a buddy told him he had "one in gazillion chances to make the team." The first time the coaches timed him at forty yards, they assumed the stopwatch was wrong and made him run again. Once again, he ran a 4.5-second time, the fastest at the tryout. Although Papale survived twelve brutal days of two-day practices and made three player cuts, no one on the team took Vince seriously—that is until he made the final roster in early September.

On September 19, 1976, thirty-year-old Vince Papale became the oldest rookie to ever play in the National Football League. In a made-for-Hollywood moment, Papale ran the length of the field when the Eagles came out of the locker room. He stopped in the end zone and pointed to Section 724, where his dad and his "a gazillion to one" buddy were going crazy. During the fourth quarter, Papale returned a fumble for a touchdown, clinching Vermeil's first win for the Eagles.

Vince Papale played three seasons for the Eagles, mostly on special teams. In his second season, his teammates elected him as special teams captain because of his kamikaze–style play. He played like a guy who did not know how long his career would last. When the movie Rocky premiered in 1976, the Eagles fans were already cheering for their Rocky Balboa in football cleats.

"Vince Papale was a thirty-year-old rookie with no right to be on the team," said Dick Vermeil. "He only got invited to training camp to fill out the numbers. We signed a local schoolteacher to a football contract and his tough, hard-nosed, don't tell me I can't do it attitude inspired a whole city." Vermeil would go on to take the Philadelphia Eagles to the Super Bowl XV where they lost to the Oakland Raiders.

Today Vince and his wife, Janet, a former member of the 1970-73 U.S. World gymnastics team, live in Cherry Hill, New Jersey. Vince retired from Sallie Mae Bank where he was a Senior Account Executive.

He remains a diehard Eagles fan and season ticket holder.

REFERENCES

Papale, Vince. *Invincible: My Journey from Fan to NFL Team Captain*. New York: Hachette Books, September 5, 2006.

Quackenbush, Eric. "The Unembellished Story of Vince Papale." Bleacher Report. Bleacher Report, February 15, 2005. https://bleacherreport.com/articles/124531-the-unembellished-story-of-vince-papale.

"Vince Papale - Home." Vince Papale. Accessed April 1, 2022. http://www.vincepapale.com/.

TOMMY JOHN'S SURGERY

"It's impossible," said pride. "It's risky," said experience. "It's pointless," said reason. "Give it a try," whispered the heart.
Unknown

July 1974 – Los Angeles, California: Los Angeles Dodgers pitcher Tommy John peppered team orthopedic surgeon Frank Jobe with questions. "Is there any chance that I can pitch again? Is there anything that can be done?" Jobe shook his head. But he described a new experimental surgery in which a tendon from another part of the body was being used to repair ligament damage in the feet and knees. It had never been tried on a baseball pitcher's elbow before.

Jobe thought he might be able to take a tendon from John's left forearm and replace the ligament. John asked, "What are my chances of pitching without surgery?" Jobe told him, "No chance." John persisted, "And if I have the surgery?" "Maybe one in a hundred," was the doctor's response.

A coach of his once said, "Tommy John would rather die than quit." Tommy John had no quit in him. Though he was an excellent high school baseball pitcher and basketball player, teammates joked that John could not break a pane of glass with his fastball. Despite his lack of velocity, the soft-throwing southpaw won twenty-eight games and lost only two at Gerstmeyer High School in Terre Haut, Indiana.

After high school, John turned down a basketball scholarship to Kentucky and, to the surprise of many, signed a baseball contract with the Cleveland Indians. In 1963, twenty-year-old John with a mediocre 86-mile-per-hour fastball became a starting pitcher for the Indians after just two minor league seasons.

Over the next eleven seasons, John won 146 games with Cleveland, the Chicago White Sox, and Los Angeles Dodgers. By the 1974 season, sporting a 13-3 record with the Los Angeles Dodgers, John had become one of the best pitchers in baseball.

On July 17, 1974, while pitching against the Montreal Expos, John heard a pop and felt a sharp pain in this left elbow. Diagnostic tests revealed a torn ulnar collateral ligament, the most common career-ending injury to pitchers.

After the discussion with Jobe about his chances to pitch again, John opted to have the surgery. In a four-hour surgery, Dr. Jobe made holes in the humerus and ulna bones of John's left elbow and used anchors to insert the tendon in what was roughly a figure-eight shape. As a result, John missed the entire 1975 season. It took eighteen long months before he could throw a baseball again. He pushed himself in his daily workouts. There were plenty of times when he wondered if he would ever play again.

During the low points, John hung his hope on a verse from Luke: "For nothing shall be impossible with God." In 1976, he finally returned to the Dodgers. His 10-10 won-loss record earned him the National League Comeback Player of the Year award. A year later, John was a better pitcher than before the surgery. With increased velocity on his fastball, he won twenty games against seven losses.

Tommy John pitched for twelve seasons following his experimental surgery. He won 164 games, 18 more than during the 11 years before the surgery. When he finally retired in 1989 at age forty-six, the "bionic man" was the oldest player in baseball. During his 26 major league seasons, second only to Hall of Famer pitcher Nolan Ryan's 27 seasons, John won 288 games, played in four all-star games, and pitched in four World Series with the Dodgers and New York Yankees.

Today, Dr. Jobe's revolutionary surgery is known as Tommy John surgery. More than 500 major league pitchers have had the surgery to extend their careers. With a ninety percent success rate, it has become the surgery of choice for baseball players to overcome what was once a career-ending injury.

REFERENCES

Baseball Almanac. "Tommy John Baseball Stats." Baseball Almanac, Inc. Accessed April 1, 2022. https://www.baseball-almanac.com/players/player.php?p=johnto01.

Cormier, Roger. "Who Is Tommy John, and Why Is There a Surgery Named after Him?" Mental Floss, June 3, 2016. https://www.mentalfloss.com/article/80317/who-tommy-john-and-why-there-surgery-named-after-him.

Fallon, Michael. "Tommy John." Society for American Baseball Research, June 28, 2011. https://sabr.org/bioproj/person/tommy-john/.

Holiday, Ryan. *Obstacle is the Way: The Timeless Art of Turning Trials into Triumphs.* New York: Portfolio Publishing, May 1, 2014, See "Story of Tommy John", 40-44.

THE SHOTS HEARD 'ROUND THE WORLD

"The young do not know enough to be prudent, and therefore they attempt the impossible—and achieve it generation after generation."
Pearl S. Buck

September 21, 1913 - U.S. Open Golf Tournament - Brookline, Massachusetts: It was the kind of moment that boys dream about or dread. To try to put the incredible win into perspective, imagine the World Series happening across the street from your house, and you are asked to pitch game seven, and you are the winning pitcher.

Or imagine that the NFL Super Bowl is occurring in your neighborhood, and you quarterback the winning team to victory. Such was the moment for a gangly twenty-year-old amateur golfer playing in the 1913 U.S. Open Golf Tournament across the street from his house in Brookline.

For what seemed like forever, Francis Ouimet, with his ten-year-old caddie Eddie Lowery by his side, stood studying his fifteen-foot birdie putt on hole number seventeen, the hole directly across from his house. He had a two-stroke lead in a sudden-death playoff round against four-time British Open Champion Harry Vardon. Experts and critics alike had fully expected young David to succumb to Goliath long before now.

Several thousand people gathered on hole number seventeen, including Francis' mother, Mary Ellen, who had never seen him play golf, but who had slipped across the street to watch the events unfold on this late afternoon. Now she held her breath along with the crowd and prayed silently. Ouimet confidently stroked the putt and the roar of the hometown crowd was heard for several miles. He went on to win the tournament and stun the golfing world. No amateur golfer had ever won the U.S. Open.

When Francis Ouimet was four years old, his parents bought a house in Brookline across the street from the seventeenth hole at The Country Club Golf Course, the oldest golf course in America, but the Ouimets did not have the money to join the country club. Francis and his older brother caddied for golfers to make spending money. The two brothers created a three-hole golf course in their backyard using sunken tomato cans for the cups and taught themselves to play golf with an old club they found.

Francis' golf skills caught the attention of the course caddie master who allowed him to play the course during less busy periods. Francis' father encouraged him to "give up golf and do something worthwhile with his life." By his late teens, Francis had made a name for himself by winning several local tournaments. Encouraged by his win in the Massachusetts State Amateur Championship in the spring of 1913, Francis decided to try to enter the U.S. Open.

After qualifying for the U.S. Open, no easy feat, Francis had to convince his boss to grant him two days off from his job at a sporting goods store. Despite his youth and inexperience, he matched the seasoned veteran Vardon stroke for stroke in the first three rounds of the tournament. Incredibly, after sinking the putt on number seventeen, Francis calmly birdied the final hole of the tournament and beat Vardon by four strokes.

Francis Ouimet's victory ended Britain's domination of the golf world, and his improbable victory transformed the interest in golf across the nation. In 1913, there were an estimated 350,000 golfers in the U.S. but, inspired by Ouimet's impossible win, just ten years later the number was up to two million golfers.

Although unquestionably less revolutionary than the "shots heard round the world" which began the Revolutionary War at Lexington, Massachusetts, 138 years earlier, the shots fired on September 21, 1913, on a golf course twelve miles away revolutionized the game of golf. The young kid whose father discouraged him from playing golf will forever be known as the Father of American Golf.

REFERENCES

Francis Ouimet Scholarship Fund. "Francis Ouimet Shocks the World at the 1913 U.S. Open!" YouTube. May 21, 2013. https://www.youtube.com/watch?v=44QTNKS01K8.

Francis Ouimet Scholarship Fund, December 15, 2021. http://www.ouimet.org/.

"In Play: Francis Ouimet Centennial." Golf Channel. Accessed April 1, 2022. https://www.golfchannel.com/video/play-francis-ouimet-centennial.

"World Golf Hall of Fame Members 1.8.13." Accessed April 2, 2022. http://www.worldgolfhalloffame.org/wp-content/uploads/2013/03/Hall-of-Fame-Members-by-Year.pdf.

THE HUMAN VACUUM CLEANER

"Adversity is preparation for greatness."
Andy Andrews

May 18, 1959 – Baltimore, Maryland: On Brooks Robinson's twenty-second birthday, Baltimore Orioles Manager Paul Richards invited the young third baseman to breakfast. Robinson was excited about breakfast with the skipper and anticipated a birthday wish and affirmation of his bright future in the organization.

Instead, Robinson received the shock of his life. Richards told Robinson that he had been assigned to the Orioles Triple A team in Vancouver, British Columbia. It was the worst birthday of Robinson's life. His dreams were shattered, his ego crushed, and he was just plain scared.

A Little Rock, Arkansas native, Brooks' father played semipro baseball and, in 1937, was on the International Harvester team that went to the finals of the World Softball Championship. Inspired by his father, at the age of five, young Brooks was hitting rocks in the yard with a sawed-off broomstick.

In the eighth grade, he wrote an English composition entitled, "Why I Want to Play Professional Baseball," and in it stated that he wanted to play third base for the St. Louis Cardinals. In 1955, on the day he graduated from high school, Brooks signed a baseball contract with the Baltimore Orioles and reported to their minor league team at York, Pennsylvania.

On Opening Day 1957, after only two seasons in the minor league, Brooks started at third base for the Orioles. Two weeks later, he had knee surgery, was out for two months, and was sent to the minor league to rehab. In 1958, Robinson spent the entire season in Baltimore but struggled at the plate batting only 0.238. The first full year in the majors had been a learning experience for Robinson, and he returned to spring training in 1959 full of hope and high expectations.

After Brooks dream-busting birthday breakfast with Richards, he was at rock bottom. He knew that when a player was sent back to the minor leagues they were forgotten. His high school scouting report dominated his thoughts. It read, "Great glove, can't run, arm not that strong, will never hit in the big leagues; always cool when the chips are down."

The scouting report was spot on—Brooks was no speed demon and hitting was not his strength, but he had been referred to as a "vacuum cleaner at third base." Most importantly, he didn't get discouraged easily. His hitting had been underwhelming but knew he could learn to hit big league pitching.

Brooks arrived in Vancouver with something to prove. In 42 games there, he improved his batting average to 0.331 and was called up to Baltimore in early July. Once again, he struggled at the plate hitting only 0.183 in July, but in the final two months of the season he hit 0.340, securing his future with Baltimore.

In 1960, Brooks earned the first of an unprecedented sixteen straight Gold Glove Awards, given to the best fielding third baseman in the American League. His hitting steadily improved and, in 1964, he hit 0.317, led the league with 188 runs-batted-in, and was voted Most Valuable Player in the American League. During his career, Brooks played in eighteen All-Star games and helped lead the Orioles to six division play-offs and two World Series championships.

Brooks Robinson, the best defensive third baseman to ever play the game, dazzled fans for twenty-three seasons with his glove magic. In 1983, he was inducted into the Major League Baseball Hall of Fame and has been voted number forty-three on the "ESPN 100 Greatest Baseball Players of All Time" list.

Brooks looks back on his career commenting, "One of the worst things that ever happened to me—getting sent back to the minors on my twenty-second birthday—

turned out to be the best thing that could have happened to Brooks Robinson. Vancouver was a time of growth and development for me after a setback. Vancouver was my springboard for All-Star appearances, World Series games, and my eventual induction into the baseball Hall of Fame."

REFERENCES

Andrews, Andy. *Storms of Perfection, Volume 1.* Lightning Crown Publishers, June 1991. See "Brooks Robinson Letter."

"Brooks Robinson." Baseball Hall of Fame. Accessed April 1, 2022. https://admin.baseballhall.org/hall-of-famers/robinson-brooks.

"Brooks Calbert Robinson Jr. (1937–)." Encyclopedia of Arkansas, April 27, 2021. https://encyclopediaofarkansas.net/entries/brooks-calbert-robinson-jr-2520/.

Kates, Maxwell. "Brooks Robinson." Society for American Baseball Research, October 6, 2021. https://sabr.org/bioproj/person/brooks-robinson/.

GETTING BACK UP

"The first thing I teach skaters at my skating academy is how to get up, because we're going to fall. It's how you get up... because the more times you get up, the stronger you are to face the next thing, which will happen, because that's life."
Scott Hamilton

August 28, 1958 – Toledo, Ohio: A five pound baby boy came into the world on a late August afternoon. There were no records of his birth mother. Six weeks later, Dorothy and Ernest Hamilton adopted the baby and named him Scott. After suffering through three miscarriages following the birth of a daughter, the Hamiltons, who were teachers in Bowling Green, Kentucky, were thrilled about their new baby.

At age four, Scott struggled with respiratory and stomach ailments and stopped growing. Numerous visits to specialists were unsuccessful in diagnosing the illness. The doctors gave Scott six months to live, and the Hamilton's search grew more desperate. They finally found help at the Boston Children's Hospital where Scott was diagnosed with Schwachman syndrome, a rare pancreas disorder characterized by small stature and difficulty in absorbing food. With the aid of medication, Scott's condition was stabilized, and he began to put on weight.

When Scott was eight, a neighbor invited him to go ice-skating. Concerned about his frail health, Dorothy initially said no, but then reluctantly consented to let him go. That day, when Scott strapped on the skates, he found his passion. He begged to go to the rink each week and Dorothy took him, happy that he came alive on the ice and that his health was improving.

By eleven, Scott was spending hours in training and winning figure skating competitions. Two years later, the Hamiltons took out a second mortgage on their house so Scott could move to Rockton, Illinois, to train more intensively. Dorothy often told friends and family, "Someday, Scottie is going to be in the Olympics."

In 1975, Dorothy was diagnosed with breast cancer and had to quit her job. The Hamiltons could no longer support seventeen-year-old Scott's training, and he was forced to move back home. Dorothy's death two years later lit a fire under Scott. He found sponsors to help with expenses and returned to Rockton.

In 1980, Scott made the U.S. Olympic figure skating team. The 5-foot-2 skater was chosen to carry the flag when the team marched into the stadium in Lake Placid, New York. Scott finished fifth in the competition, but one year later, he won the World Figure Skating Championship and went on to win the gold medal in the 1984 Olympics in Sarajevo, Yugoslavia.

After winning the gold, Scott became a pro skater and cofounded the touring production *Stars on Ice*. He also worked as a figure skating commentator. In 1990, he was inducted into the U.S. Olympic and World Figure Skating Halls of Fame.

In 1997, while skating with *Stars on Ice*, Scott was diagnosed with testicular cancer. Following chemotherapy, he resumed skating until retiring in 2001. Three years later he had surgery to remove a benign pituitary tumor. The tumor returned in 2010 and was once again removed.

In 2016, 58-year-old Scott was diagnosed with a brain tumor for the third time. When Scott's wife, Tracie, learned of the diagnosis, she did not say anything; instead, she took both his hands in hers and started praying. On Scott's next visit to the doctor, there was no sign of a tumor.

When the surgeon was asked to explain it, he shrugged, "God, that's it." About the ups and downs in his life, Scott laughs, "I have a unique hobby. I collect life-threatening illnesses. God doesn't owe me a day. I'm good. Whatever's next is next. In everything I do, I celebrate life."

The Hamiltons have two biological children and two adopted Haitian children. They live in Franklin, Tennessee, where Scott operates a skating academy.

REFERENCES

Batura, Paul. *Chosen for Greatness: How Adoption Changes the World.* Washington, D. C.: Regnery Faith Publishing, November 1, 2016.

McKenzie, Joi-Marie. "Former Olympic Figure Skater Scott Hamilton Diagnosed with Third Brain Tumor." *ABC News,* October 23, 2016.

"Olympic Skater Scott Hamilton Reveals 'Spectacular Miracle' Surrounding Battle with His Third Brain Tumor." *Christian Broadcasting Network News,* March 18, 2017.

"Scott Hamilton." Biography.com. A&E Networks Television, April 23, 2021. https://www.biography.com/athlete/scott-hamilton.

COACH CHANGE

"I probably cost Tennessee two national championships early in my career because I was too stubborn to change."
Pat Summitt

1974 – University of Tennessee – Knoxville, Tennessee: After graduating from the University of Tennessee at Martin, 22-year-old Pat Head became the assistant basketball coach at the University of Tennessee. When the head coach quit soon after she arrived, the athletic director gave Pat the job and a $250 per month salary. Four of her players were her age. Her job included driving the team van, cleaning the gym, and washing the team uniforms which were bought with the proceeds from donuts sales. Pat was in over her head and made plenty of mistakes.

Pat Head was raised on a small tobacco and dairy farm in Henrietta, Tennessee. Essentially raised as her father's fourth son, she got her strength, discipline, and drive from him. By age ten, Trish, her name on the farm, was driving a tractor, planting tobacco, baling hay, and feeding the cows. The family lived from crop to crop, and everybody did their part.

Her father put up a basketball goal and a string of lights on the edge of a hayfield so his kids could play basketball at night after the work was done. Two older brothers signed basketball scholarships. Trish, who graduated high school in 1970, didn't receive one because Title IX, federal legislation requiring equity for females in sports, was still five years away.

Pat was an outstanding basketball player at the University of Tennessee at Martin, earning All-American honors. In 1976, she played forward on the inaugural women's basketball team which won a silver medal in Montreal.

As the new coach at Tennessee, Pat was extremely demanding of herself and her players. According to the folks in Henrietta, "That was just her daddy in her." She expected her players to exceed their potential, and she was never satisfied with the status quo. Pat's notorious ice-cold, blue-eyed stare could bore right into the soul of a player. It took Pat six years to win her first SEC Championship in 1980. That same year she married R.B. Summitt, a Knoxville banker.

Pat's first national championship came in 1987. She won three straight National Championships in 1996-98 and her 1998 team, which went 39-0, is considered by many to be the best women's college basketball team in history.

In August 2011, the 59-year-old coach was diagnosed with Alzheimer's. Just as she had with any opponent she faced, Pat battled the disease with fierce determination. However, she coached only one more season, winning her sixteenth SEC Championship.

With 1,098 wins, Pat Summitt is the winningest coach in NCAA basketball history for both men and women. She won sixteen SEC Championships and eight NCAA women's basketball championships during her 38-year career at Tennessee. In 2000, Pat was voted the Naismith Basketball Coach of the Century, and she is number eleven on the Sporting News 50 Greatest Coaches of All-time.

Pat Summitt's success at Tennessee, perhaps more than any other coach, put women's sports on the front page. The most successful college basketball coach in history attributes her success to continual change and improvement. "Without changing something every year, we would never have won all these national championships. The willingness to experiment with change may be the most essential ingredient to success at anything."

On Tuesday, June 28, 2016, 64-year-old Patricia Summitt died peacefully at the Sherrill Hill Senior Living Facility in Knoxville, Tennessee. Her time on earth was far too short, but her legacy will be felt for generations.

REFERENCES

Berlinger, Joshua and Willingham, A. J. "Pat Summitt, Legendary Women's Basketball Coach, Dies at 64." CNN, June 28, 2016.

Summitt, Pat, with Jenkins, Sally. *Reach for the Summitt.* Portland: Broadway Books, 1998.

Voepel, Mechelle, "There Will Never Be Anyone Like Tennessee Legend Pat Summitt." ESPN, June 28, 2016.

THE GAME THAT CHANGED COLLEGE BASKETBALL

"The fact of being an underdog changes people in ways that we often fail to appreciate. It opens doors and creates opportunities and enlightens and permits things that might otherwise have seemed unthinkable."
Malcolm Gladwell

March 19, 1966 – University of Maryland – College Park, Maryland: The game was voted the biggest upset in NCAA basketball championship history. It may be the most significant college basketball game ever played. If there was ever a "David meets Goliath" matchup in the finals, this was it.

The game played at Cole Field House on this spring evening pitted unknown Texas Western College (now the University of Texas at El Paso) versus a basketball blue blood, the University of Kentucky. Nobody gave the Miners a chance versus the 27-1 Wildcats.

Coached by the legendary Adolph Rupp, the number one ranked Wildcats had won four national championships, twenty-five conference championships, and 750 games during Rupp's thirty-six seasons. Texas Western was making only its third tournament appearance in school history.

Two years after Dr. Martin Luther King's "I Have a Dream" speech, the 1965-66 season had been a long and challenging road for Texas Western. Opposing fans peppered the players with racial slurs during the season because of the team's seven Black players. Officials often failed to call fouls against the other team. Texas Western's only loss of the season was to the University of Seattle—a game in which the officials did not call a single foul on Seattle.

Despite being 25-3 the previous season, the Miners were left out of the preseason rankings. With a record of 17-1, the tournament's Cinderella team shocked Kansas 81-80 in the Final Four. It was a foregone conclusion that the other Final Four game between Kentucky and Duke was the real championship game. Kentucky beat Duke 83-79.

Texas Western featured four white players in additions to the seven Black players. Coach Don Haskins surprised everyone when he started five Black players in the biggest game in school history. No major college team had ever started five Black players in a game. The prevailing college basketball culture was that at least one white starter was necessary for success. Kentucky had never even recruited a Black player in school history.

Texas Western was expected to play a run-and-gun style offense, but that was not the case. The Miners brought the ball up the court slowly, ran a disciplined offense, and played tenacious defense. Led by All-Americans guards Louis Dampier and Pat Riley, Kentucky preferred to run up and down the court at every opportunity, but they had few opportunities on this night.

A quiet crowd of 14,200 mostly Kentucky fans watched the Miners jump out to a 16-11 lead with nine minutes left in the first half and never trail for the remainder of the game. They stifled the high-scoring Wildcat offense to capture an inconceivable 72-65 championship win.

Following the championship, Coach Haskins received threatening phone calls and letters because he did not play any white players. Newspapers accused him of trying to make a political statement. Those familiar with Haskins knew he would have played five kids from Mars if that were what it took to win. The team was not invited to the White House following their National Championship, even though the President, Lyndon Johnson, was a Texan.

The Texas Western players were concerned about winning a championship, not changing history, but that is ultimately what they did. Their upset win not only stunned the college basketball world, but it also went against conventional wisdom and changed basketball forever in the South. In 1967, Vanderbilt University signed the first Black player in Southeastern Conference history, and two years later Kentucky integrated its basketball team.

According to Texas Western forward Nevil Shed, "We never thought of ourselves as pioneers, never thought that we were about to change the era of college basketball. We were just a bunch of kids trying to win a championship. Coach Haskins simply put the best team out there that he could." In 1967 Coach Don Haskins and all Texas Western team members were inducted into the Naismith College Basketball Hall of Fame.

REFERENCES

Fitzpatrick, Frank. "Texas Western's 1966 Title Left a Lasting Legacy." *ESPN Classic*, November 19, 2003.

Forgrave, Reid. "50 Years Ago, Texas Western Didn't Realize What It Set in Motion." *Fox Sports*, February 5, 2016. https://www.foxsports.com/stories/college-basketball/50-years-ago-texas-western-didnt-realize-what-it-set-in-motion.

Solomon, Jon. "Significance of Texas Western's 1966 Title not Realized at First." *CBS Sports,* February 26, 2016.

"Texas Western Upsets Kentucky for N.C.A.A. Title." Kentucky vs. Texas Western (March 19, 1966). Accessed April 2, 2022. http://www.bigbluehistory.net/bb/Statistics/Games/19660319TexasWestern.html.

Wetzel, Dan. "The Long and Winding Road." *Yahoo Sports*, January 12, 2006.

DREAM BIG AND NEVER QUIT

"The process is the same for any dream. Focus on your dream. Then understand the priority of the steps to get it. Then never, ever, ever let it go. The real question is how bad do you want it? Regardless of your background, your grades, or your size, find a way."
Rudy Ruettiger

1966 – Joliet, Illinois: The guidance counselor peered at Rudy Ruettiger, "Look, you are a marginal student. You don't have the grades to get in Joliet Community College, much less Notre Dame." She encouraged him to join the military after high school. Although Rudy led the Joliet Catholic High School football team in tackles his senior season, at 5-foot-6 and 160 pounds, his dream of playing football at Notre Dame was crazy.

Rudy grew up in a large Catholic family, the third of fourteen children. His father sometimes worked two jobs to put food on the table. As far as the Ruettigers were concerned, Notre Dame was the only college football team to cheer for.

After the discussion with the guidance counselor, Rudy gave up on Notre Dame and enlisted in the Navy, where he served two years doing clerical work on a communications ship. After the Navy, Rudy went to work in the same steel mill where his father worked.

In the break room, a couple of years later, Rudy reminisced about his old dream with a high school buddy and coworker, Pete, in the mill. On Rudy's birthday, Pete gave him a Notre Dame jacket and encouraged him, "Rudy, you were born to wear that jacket. Give it a try."

In the summer of 1972, Pete was killed in an explosion in the mill. His tragic death inspired Rudy to quit his job and head to South Bend, Indiana. The longest of long shots, due to Notre Dame's high academic standards, the 24-year-old enrolled at Holy Cross Community College near the Notre Dame campus. He would give it his best shot and have no regrets.

A professor discovered that Rudy had a learning disorder during his freshman year and helped him change his study habits. Rudy's grades improved. After his first semester, he applied to Notre Dame but was rejected. Two subsequent applications were also turned down. In the spring of 1974, Rudy became a student at Notre Dame after his fourth application attempt.

Two months later, Rudy met with head football coach Ara Parseghian to ask for an opportunity to be a non-scholarship player. Although Parseghian was underwhelmed by Rudy's diminutive size, he was moved by his enthusiasm and gave him a chance. Rudy made the practice squad. As a defensive end, he was a blocking dummy for four years, but he didn't care. He was a Notre Dame football player.

Near the end of his senior season, Rudy had one final dream. He pleaded with new head coach Dan Devine to let him dress out in his last home game. Devine told him there was no way, but he changed his mind when several players volunteered to let Rudy dress in their place.

On November 8, 1975, Rudy Ruettiger wore number forty-five when Notre Dame hosted Georgia Tech in their final home game. Before the game, Notre Dame students learned of Rudy's story in the student newspaper. With three minutes left in the game, they began to chant for Rudy to enter the game.

In the final minute, number forty-five went into the game at defensive end, and in a dreams-do-come-true-moment, Rudy made a tackle for a loss on the game's final play. Jubilant teammates carried him off the field on their shoulders as the crowd continued to chant his name.

Although his Notre Dame playing career lasted only twenty-seven seconds, Rudy's never-give-up story was captured in the 1993 Hollywood movie Rudy. More than fifty years after Rudy Ruettiger's Notre Dame experience, his story continues to inspire millions around the world to chase their dreams regardless of the odds.

REFERENCES

Hahn, Jason Duaine. "What to Know about the Real Rudy Ruettiger, the Focus of the Classic Film Rudy." PEOPLE.com, October 13, 2020. https://people.com/sports/what-to-know-about-rudy-ruettiger/.

Margaritoff, Marco. "Why the Real-Life Story behind 'Rudy' Is Even More Inspirational than the Movie Depicted." All That's Interesting. June 11, 2021. https://allthatsinteresting.com/rudy-ruettiger.

McGee, Ryan. "The Story of Notre Dame Icon Rudy Ruettiger? It's Almost Too Good to Be True." ESPN. ESPN Internet Ventures, December 27, 2019. https://www.espn.com/college-football/story/_/id/28231473/the-story-notre-dame-icon-rudy-ruettiger-almost-too-good-true.

"Rudygear.com." rudygear.com. Accessed April 2, 2022. https://www.rudygear.com/.

Scofield, Dan. "Daniel 'Rudy' Ruettiger, Notre Dame's Famous Walk-on: The True Story." Bleacher Report. Bleacher Report, October 3, 2017. https://bleacherreport.com/articles/328263-the-true-story-of-notre-dames-famous-walk-on-daniel-rudy-reutigger.

NO REGRETS

"Never let the odds keep you from pursuing what you know in your heart you were meant to do."
Leroy "Satchel" Page

Early Spring, 1999 – Big Lake, Texas: Coach Jim Morris' baseball team wasn't very good. The Reagan County Owls had won one game in each of the past three seasons. They expected to lose. Morris urged them to chase a dream—to win the district championship—something the high school had never done.

During a pep talk after practice, a player stopped Morris mid-sentence, "What about you coach? Why are you telling us to chase our dreams, if you are not willing to do it yourself?" The 35-year-old coach had once dreamed of pitching in the big leagues. He pitched in the minors for four seasons before injuries ended his career. Morris made a promise to his players: If the team won the district, he would try out.

Jim Morris was born in Brownswood, Texas, in January 1964. A great baseball and football player, Morris was a first-round draft choice of the New York Yankees in 1982, but he turned them down. He wanted to get a college education first. Morris accepted a baseball scholarship to Angelo State University—100 miles from home.

Two years later, Morris was drafted again. This time by the Milwaukee Brewers, and this time he signed a contract. He pitched four seasons in their Class A minor league system but was plagued with injuries. After his fourth arm surgery, Morris called it quits, completed his degree at Angelo State, and became a high school baseball coach.

Morris assumed his bet with his players was safe. He was confident his dream was dead because he was not confident about a district championship. However, the team made the play-offs. In the district championship game, they scored four runs in the last inning to win. As Morris drove the excited team bus back to their school, his players reminded him of their deal.

A month after the championship in June 1999 Morris kept his promise. He expected to embarrass himself by trying out, but he drove two hours to a Tampa Bay Devil Rays tryout camp anyways. His wife had to work that day and, unbeknownst to her, Morris took their three young children with him. The scouts laughed when he arrived pushing the youngest child in a stroller.

Morris waited three hours in 100-degree heat and was the last player to try out. Tired of jokes about his age, he almost left, but didn't because of the promise he made to his team. When Morris threw the first pitch, he noticed a scout shake his radar gun. Morris wondered to himself, *Did I not even throw hard enough to register a velocity?* It got quiet when the big lefty threw ten straight pitches at 98 miles per hour.

That day when he got home, Morris had an interesting conversation with his wife, Lorri, about the kids and his day, and he got several calls from scouts that night. Would he come back in two days and pitch again? They wanted to verify his velocity. He would, he did, and later that week, Morris signed a contract with Tampa Bay.

Three months later, and eleven years after his last minor league game, on September 18, 1999 in front of his family and his high school team, Jim Morris made his major league debut on the mound for the Tampa Bay Devil Rays against the Texas Rangers in Arlington, Texas. He struck out the first batter he faced. Lorri cried.

Jim Morris—a 35-year-old chemistry teacher with an old dream and a 98 miles per hour fastball—became the oldest player in thirty years to make his major league debut. He was a relief pitcher for two seasons with Tampa Bay and the Los Angeles Dodgers. Although he only pitched in 21 games, Jim Morris fulfilled a promise, achieved a dream and inspired countless baseball fans around the world.

REFERENCES

Goalcast. "The Unbelievable True Story of Baseball's Oldest Rookie/Jim Morris Motivational Speech/ Goalcast." YouTube, 8:12, April 17, 2018, https://www.youtube.com/watch?v=TmOUAcGW_1E.

"Jim 'The Rookie' Morris." Facts, Video, *Jim "The Rookie" Morris*, Accessed November 5, 2020, https://www.jimtherookiemorris.com/.

Morris, Jim. "Jim Morris Biography." *Web Solutions LLC.*, Accessed November 5, 2020, https://sports.jrank.org/pages/3337/Morris-Jim.html.

O'Shea, Tyler. "Jim "The Rookie" Morris on Living Your Dreams." *Joker Magazine,* June 20, 2019, www.jokermagazine.com.

Wikipedia. "Jim Morris." Last modified August 14, 2020, https://en.wikipedia.org/wiki/Jim_Morris.

FROM SKINNY SOPHOMORE TO G.O.A.T.

"Being defeated is often a temporary condition. Giving up is what makes it permanent."
Marilyn Vos Savant

November 1978 – Wilmington, North Carolina: The basketball player universally acknowledged as the greatest of all time (G.O.A.T.) almost quit the game as a skinny fifteen-year-old. He thought about it; he talked to his father about it, but he didn't. He stuck it out. He had something to prove. This is his story.

Michael came in from school, went directly to his bedroom and slammed the door. He buried his face in the pillow. He had not made the fifteen-man roster on the Laney High School varsity basketball team. And to make matters worse, his best friend, six-foot, five-inch sophomore Leroy Smith, did.

Michael decided to quit basketball and focus on baseball. He was a more accomplished baseball player and besides, it was the sport his father loved. When

James Jordan got home and heard the story, he advised his son to give the decision a few days.

Michael Jordan was born in Brooklyn, New York in 1963, but grew up in Wilmington. An excellent athlete, he played baseball, basketball, and football in high school. As a pitcher, he would later throw forty-five consecutive shutout innings for Laney High.

In the fall of 1978, Laney basketball coach Clifton Herring's varsity basketball team returned eleven seniors and three juniors, including eight guards. What he needed was height, and at five feet, ten inches, and 160 pounds, Michael Jordan wasn't what he needed. But Herring also saw potential and wanted his promising sophomore to get more seasoning on the junior varsity.

Michael followed his father's advice and didn't quit the basketball team. He starred on the junior varsity team, twice scoring more than forty points. Two years and seven inches later, the six-foot, five-inch senior averaged twenty-seven points per game, leading the Laney High Bucs varsity team to a 19-4 record and the state playoffs. Recognized as one of the best players in the country, Michael was chosen to play in the McDonald's High School All American game and led all scorers with thirty points.

College basketball scholarship letters filled the Jordan's mailbox. Michael chose the University of North Carolina which was two hours from home. As a freshman in 1982, he led the Tar Heels to the National Championship, sinking the game-winning shot at the buzzer to beat Georgetown University. Michael was an All American his sophomore and junior years, earning college basketball player of the year honors as a junior.

In 1984, the Chicago Bulls made Michael Jordan the number three overall pick in the NBA draft. During a fifteen-year career, he led the Bulls to six NBA championships—each time being selected as the most valuable player (MVP).

His career accomplishments are unmatched and legendary: Five-time NBA MVP, ten-time All-NBA first-team selection, fourteen-time NBA All Star and ten NBA season scoring titles.

Michael retired with the NBA's highest career scoring average of thirty points per game. In 2009, he was voted into the NBA Hall of Fame. ESPN named him the greatest athlete of the twentieth century. Michael Jordan has been featured on the cover of Sports Illustrated over fifty times—more than anyone in history.

"When I got cut from the varsity basketball team as a sophomore in high school, I learned something," Jordan remembered. "I knew that I never wanted to feel that bad again. I never wanted that taste in my mouth, that hole in my stomach. I didn't quit. I set a goal of becoming a starter on the varsity as a junior. I had something to prove." And prove it, he did.

REFERENCES

Cook, Bob. "The Reality Behind the Myth of the Coach Who Cut Michael Jordan." *Forbes Magazine*, January 10, 2012.

Mazique, Brian. "Michael Jordan's High School Coach Exposes Another MJ Myth." *Bleacher Report*, January 11, 2012, https://bleacherreport.com/articles/1020151-michael-jordans-high-school-coach-exposes-another-mj-myth.

"Michael Jordan - High School, Amateur, and Exhibition Stats." *Basketball Reference*, Accessed December 16, 2020, https://www.basketball-reference.com/players/j/jordami01/jordan-high-school-amateur-exhibition.

Newsweek Special Edition. "Michael Jordan Didn't Make Varsity—At First." Culture Newsweek, October 17, 2015, https://www.newsweek.com/missing-cut-382954.

Wikipedia. "Michael Jordan." Last updated December 16, 2020, https://en.wikipedia.org/wiki/Michael_Jordan.

NO. 23

"God is always working on our behalf, behind the scenes where we can't fully see. In that place where we see no way out, in that struggle where we see no solution, in that problem where we have no answer. He knows our way and has a plan."
Debbie McDaniel

1968 – Dallas, Texas: "Talk to your grandmother?" asked SMU football coach Hayden Fry. Jerry LeVias responded, "The line was busy." The game with TCU was ten minutes from kickoff, but Fry had made a promise. He borrowed a quarter from a band member and the two of them placed a call on a payphone under the stands to Ella LeVias in Beaumont, Texas. As was her practice, she prayed for them.

Jerry LeVias grew up in Beaumont, Texas, in a home where education was more important than sports. Jerry's father didn't get an education, and he was determined that Jerry would. Although small, Jerry was an outstanding football player. When he graduated from Hebert High School in 1965, he had more than seventy football and academic scholarships. It was a year after the Civil Rights Act was signed, and none of the offers were from the Deep South. Jerry decided to play football at UCLA like his older cousin Mel Pharr.

Near the end of the 1965 recruiting period, three cars pulled up in the LeVias' driveway. Jerry's high school coach and five white guys got out. Inquisitive neighbors stood on the front porch, assuming Jerry was in trouble with the police.

Hayden Fry had done his homework. He went next door to Jerry's grandmother's house while the other men went to the LeVias house. In 1962, when 36-year-old Fry took the job at SMU, he told SMU President Willis Tate he would recruit Black players if he ever got the opportunity.

Coach Fry spent thirty minutes with Ella LeVias before going next door. She had two requests of Fry: allow Jerry to wear number twenty-three, her favorite Psalm, and make Jerry call her before every game so she could pray for him. She knew he would need to be a warrior like David. Fry was the only coach who talked to Jerry and his family about the importance of education. When Jerry visited SMU, he spent his time with professors, not the coaching staff.

When Jerry LeVias became the first Black player at SMU and the first in the Southwest Conference, he walked a lonely road. Most of the players did not want him there. Nobody would room with Jerry during his four years at SMU. He showered by himself. On the first day of class, he sat in a row by himself. There was enormous verbal and physical abuse and even death threats on several occasions. Coach Fry faithfully called Jerry every night to check on him. He made Jerry's loneliness more bearable.

At the SMU President's request, Dr. Martin Luther King Jr. visited the campus in Dallas in March 1966 and spoke to a packed McFarlin Auditorium crowd. Afterward, Jerry had the opportunity to visit with him. Dr. King reminded Jerry of what his grandmother always told him, "Even if they cuss, hit, or spit on you, always keep your emotions under control. Keep your composure even when others don't."

There were plenty of times Jerry thought about quitting. He called his sister in California during his first year and told her he was coming to UCLA. She reminded Jerry of what their father said. "You gave Coach Fry your word. You make your bed. You sleep in it." Jerry had made his bed at SMU.

Jerry LeVias' tenacity paid off. In the fall of 1966, the 5-foot-9 wide receiver led the Mustangs to their first conference championship in eighteen years. Number twenty-three would go on to be a three-time All-Southwest Conference choice. As a senior, he was voted All-America and Academic All-American. Jerry played six years in the National Football League before a successful career with Continental Oil as a sales executive. In 2003, Jerry was inducted into the College Football Hall of Fame.

Jerry LeVias was a pioneer for other Black football players. His success took a committed coach, a praying grandmother, and plenty of patience and determination.

REFERENCES

Dunnavant, Keith. *American Achievers Podcast.* An Interview with Jerry LeVias, January 17, 2022.

Payne, Arnold. "A Living Hell: Jerry LeVias, First Black Scholarship Athlete at SMU, Describes Treatment on the Football Field." *WFAA Television,* Dallas, Texas, October 19, 2020.

Sherrington, Kevin. "Jerry LeVias made history at SMU with help from Hayden Fry, but it was never easy." *Dallas Morning News,* December 18, 2019

"SMU Athletics Scoreboard: Jerry Levias." SMU Athletics. Accessed April 2, 2022. https://smumustangs.com/honors/hall-of-fame/jerry-levias/48.

THE SHOE SALESMAN

"Seek your calling even if you don't know what it means. If you are following your calling, the fatigue will be easier to bear, the disappointments will be fuel."
Phil Knight

1962 – Portland, Oregon: "I didn't send you to college to be a door-to-door shoe salesman," William Knight complained to his son Phil. "When are you going to quit messing with those shoes?" Phil shrugged his shoulders. His college professor thought his idea "a little crazy," nevertheless, he had given Phil an "A" on his term paper.

After earning three letters on the track team and a journalism degree from the University of Oregon, followed by a Stanford University MBA, 24-year-old Phil Knight was living back at home. He spent most of his time obsessing over a graduate school term paper that he had written. Phil predicted Japan would capture the U.S. athletic shoe market just as the Sony Corporation had taken over camera technology. His father, the editor of the *Oregon Journal*, wanted his son to become a journalist, but Phil's passion for sports drove him to become an entrepreneur.

He used his savings and flew to visit the Onitsuka Company, the maker of Tiger athletic shoes in Kobe, Japan. Despite not having his own company, Phil persuaded Onitsuka to allow him to represent Tiger shoes on the West Coast. He ordered 300 pairs of track shoes at $3.33 each and flew back to Oregon to figure out how to raise $1,000 before the shoes arrived.

Phil's old Oregon track coach, Bill Bowerman, who had been experimenting with track shoe designs, loaned him $500. Phil's father loaned him the rest of the money despite his initial concerns. In April 1964, when the first shoe shipment arrived, Phil's mother bought the first pair. He sold Tigers out of his parent's living room and at high school and college track meets from the trunk of his lime-green Plymouth Valiant.

Phil sold his first order by July and ordered 900 more pairs. After depleting his father's reserve cash account of $3,000, Phil was informed that the Bank of Dad was closed. He sold $8,000 worth of Tiger shoes by the end of 1964.

In 1965, Phil started Blue Ribbon Sports in his parents' basement, and a year later, he opened his first retail store in Portland. To help pay the bills, he got a job as an accountant with Price Waterhouse. Phil spent his nights and weekends at Blue Ribbon. When he told his boss at Price Waterhouse that he was starting a running shoe company, the boss asked, "Why the hell would you do something like that?"

By 1971, annual shoe sales reached $750,000, and Phil received a three-year contract extension from Onitsuka. He also changed the company name to Nike, the Greek Goddess of Victory, but little did Phil know Nike was far from victory.

In late 1971, Onitsuka attempted a hostile takeover of Nike, and the bank dropped its loan. Phil saved his company by quickly moving production to an Adidas shoe factory in Guadalajara, Mexico. In 1975, Nike was on the brink of bankruptcy when a Japanese trading company agreed to a cash loan. Although annual sales continued to climb, the company operated month-to-month on fragile lines of credit and was routinely in trouble.

Phil wrestled with the idea of taking Nike public for five years. Finally, in December 1980, he made the leap and introduced Nike to the world. Today, Nike is the world's largest athletic apparel company. Its renowned "swoosh" is among the most recognizable brands in the world. Headquartered in Beaverton, Oregon, the company employs 75,000 people, and their popular athletic gear is sold in 5,000 stores worldwide.

Phil Knight retired as CEO of Nike in 2015 at age seventy-seven. His net worth places him among the Top 25 Richest People in the world. Oregonians are known for blazing a trail across the country in covered wagons in the 1830s, and 130 years later a young door-to-door shoe salesman in Portland blazed a trail into the running shoe world when most thought he was crazy.

REFERENCES

Golden, Jessica. "How Phil Knight turned a Dream into a $25 Billionaire Fortune." *CNBC*, May 9, 2016.

Knight, Phil. *Shoe Dog—A Memoir by the Creator of Nike*. New York: Scribner Publishing, 2016.

Martin, Emmie. "How Phil Knight Built Nike into one of the Biggest Brands in the World and Became a Billionaire." *Business Insider*, August 23, 2015.

THE SUGAR LAND EXPRESS

"Kenneth Hall was the biggest coaching mistake I ever made. You're a fool to think you can treat them all alike. He should have been an All-American. With him, we would have won the 1957 National Championship. Without him, we lost."
Coach Bear Bryant

Fall 1954, Texas A&M University – College Station, Texas: They nicknamed him the "Sugar Land Express." Ken Hall arrived on campus as the best high school football player in history. The single-wing formation quarterback at Sugar Land High School set seventeen national rushing records from 1950-53. In a game against Houston Lutheran High School, Hall ran for seven touchdowns, intercepted a pass, and returned a punt, both for touchdowns, and rushed for 520 yards. Sugar Land fans expected that from him.

At A&M, Hall did not fit 42-year-old first-year head coach Bear Bryant's offensive and defensive schemes or his hard-nosed football philosophy. The easy-going Hall wasn't mean enough or aggressive enough for Bryant. Tired of Bryant's constant criticism, Hall quit the team midway through his sophomore season, moved back to Sugar Land, and married his high school sweetheart.

Hall had been "Mr. Everything" for Sugar Land High. At 6-foot-1 and 205 pounds with world-class sprinter speed, he had the unique ability to be running full speed after one step. He led the school to three straight district football championships, three state track titles, and two district basketball titles. Some thought Ken Hall could have made the U.S. Olympic team in the decathlon.

In the spring of 1956, Hall had a change of heart and begged Bryant to take him back on the team. Bryant agreed, but Hall continued to be a fish out of water. Bryant believed in defense first and as little offense as was necessary to win. Bryant forced Hall, a stand-up quarterback who never blocked and rarely was tackled in high school, to play fullback and linebacker. Hall hated both positions. He never started a game for the Aggies. He quit again after the seventh game of his junior year.

In 1957, in what would have been Hall's senior year at Texas A&M, he signed a $7,000 contract to play for the Edmonton Eskimos in the Canadian Football League. Meanwhile, in College Station, John David Crowe, a halfback and classmate of Hall's, won the Heisman Trophy as the best college football player in America.

After a year in Canada, the Baltimore Colts in the National Football League drafted Hall. He also played for Pittsburg, Chicago, and Houston before a crushed vertebra in his neck prematurely ended his NFL career. His four-year NFL career proved that Hall had what it took to play at the highest level. In 1983, Hall was inducted into the High School Football Hall of Fame. In 1999, the Kenneth Hall Trophy was established and is given annually to the nation's top high school football player.

Coach Bryant always regretted that he derailed the Sugar Land Express. Before he died, and twenty-five years after Ken Hall quit his team at Texas A&M, Bryant wrote to Hall. He shared how sorry he was that things hadn't worked out at A&M and how glad he was that Hall had a successful business career. Bryant said that he learned a valuable lesson from the mistakes he had made coaching Hall: that there are different ways to motivate people and that not everyone responds to constant pressure and badgering. And Bryant admitted that Hall was a better running back than John David Crowe.

Ken Hall, by then a successful business executive with an artificial sweetener company near San Francisco, was surprised to receive the letter. He graciously accepted Bryant's apology. Today, 84-year-old Hall has no regrets. More than fifty-five years later, the Sugar Land Express remains a legend in Texas football lore, still holding four Texas high school and two national rushing records.

Paul William "Bear" Bryant is arguably the greatest college football coach of all times with 323 wins and six national championships. Though he had some early success at Texas A&M, it was what he learned from his coaching blunders and his willingness to change and continuously improve that ultimately made him into one of the greatest to ever walk a college sideline.

REFERENCES

Coleman, Adam. "Sugar Land Express: Kenneth Hall ran like no other high school football player; the speedy 'Sugar Land Express' awed fans of high school football in the 1950s." *Houston Chronicle*, October 21, 2016.

Krider, Dave. "Six decades later, everyone is still chasing Texas rushing legend Ken Hall." *MaxPreps*, July 3, 2011. https://www.maxpreps.com/news/ji06H-KMyEeCkhgAcxJSkrA/six-decades-later%2C-everyone-is-still-chasing-texas-rushing-legend-ken-hall.htm.

SI Staff. "Whatever Happened to the Sugar Land Express?" *Vault Sports Illustrated*, September 27, 1982, https://vault.si.com/vault/1982/09/27/whatever-happened-to-the-sugar-land-express.

Wikipedia. "Ken Hall (American Football)." Last updated March 31, 2022. https://en.wikipedia.org/wiki/Ken_Hall_(American_football).

CLEVELAND STROUD'S INTEGRITY

"Never, never be afraid to do the right thing…society's punishments are small compared to the wounds we inflict in our soul when we look the other way."
Martin Luther King, Jr

1987 – Rockdale County High School – Conyers, Georgia: It has been thirty-five years, but people in Rockdale County still talk about Coach Cleveland Stroud and the 1987 state championship. The mementos are still there. The framed front page of *The Rockdale Citizen* with the headline, "Bulldogs King of AAA," the pictures of team members, and the autographed team basketball are still displayed in the trophy case.

Cleveland Stroud grew up in Rockdale County. He attended Morehouse College on a basketball scholarship, but when his wife Helen became pregnant, he dropped out of school and took a job as a custodian in the Rockdale County school system to support his family. Stroud worked as a janitor for eleven years until age thirty-one when, with Helen's support, he enrolled again at Morehouse. At age thirty-four, he graduated and became a teacher and basketball coach in the Rockdale County school system.

In 1987, Coach Stroud—the school's first Black head coach—began his eleventh season as basketball coach of Rockdale County High School. The Bulldogs began the season with fifteen players, but Stroud cut five players who failed to make the previous semester's grades. Despite having to move five players up from the junior varsity, Rockdale finished the season at 21-5 and made the state tournament. The Bulldogs surprised No.1 Bainbridge High in the semifinals and then had a dramatic 62-60 come-from-behind-win over Fulton in the championship game to claim the school's first basketball title.

A month after the state championship, Coach Stroud was reviewing grades on a Friday afternoon prior to spring football practice when he discovered that one of his sophomore players who moved up from the JV had been academically ineligible. The player had played for forty-five seconds in the first state tournament game when the team was leading by 23 points.

Stroud had a dilemma. If he revealed the minor infraction, his team would likely be deprived of their state championship. If he kept quiet, it was unlikely that anymore would ever discover the offense. But he knew. And if he kept quiet, his state championship would always be tainted with an ugly little secret. Stroud thought about it all weekend. He knew what he had to do. On Monday morning he was waiting in Principal Henry Gibb's office when he arrived.

"My heart hit the floor when Coach Stroud told me," Gibbs said. "But there was never any question about what we had to do. We were wrong, and we had to turn ourselves in." They reported the infraction later that day to the Georgia High School Association.

After informing the school board and the team, Gibbs and Stroud went on the school's public address system and informed the students that they were probably going to lose their state championship. Then they left campus because they didn't want the students to see them crying.

A month later, the state association stripped Rockdale County High of their championship and asked for the trophy to be returned. Many Bulldog fans were angry about the turn of events. The kid only played for forty-five seconds. He didn't even score. How could the Georgia High School Association strip the Bulldogs of their title?

Later that year, Cleveland Stroud's decision to do the right thing was recognized with numerous awards, including Conyers Citizen of the Year and Georgia High School Coach of the Year. The International Olympic Organization's Fair Play Committee's awarded Stroud and the school the prestigious Youth Fair Play Award.

"I called a team meeting and shared with them what had happened," 84-year-old Cleveland Stroud reminisces. "They can take away our trophy, and they can take away our title, but they can't take away the fact that we won. In a few years people will forget the score, and even who won, but they won't ever forget what you're made of."

In Rockdale County, Georgia, people have long sense forgotten the Bulldog's state championship details, but they have never forgotten Cleveland Stroud's integrity. Giving up the state title brought more recognition than winning the championship.

REFERENCES

Daniels, Kysa. "Coach Cleveland Stroud." *The Covington News*, October 19, 2015, https://www.covnews.com/news/coach-cleveland-stroud/.

Queen, Alice. "Conyers City Council member Cleveland Stroud closes out 28-year tenure." *The Citizens,* December 16, 2021. https://www.rockdalenewtoncitizen.com/news/conyers-city-council-member-cleveland-stroud-closes-out-28-year-tenure/article_f7bc440c-5e77-11ec-ac8b-7fb9b5a75ac5.html.

Schmidt, William. "For Town and Team, Honor Is Its Own Reward." Special to *The New York Times*, May 25, 1987, https://www.nytimes.com/1987/05/25/us/for-town-and-team-honor-is-its-own-reward.html.

Staff Reporter. "School board to name gym after former coach." *The Citizens,* October 29, 2012, https://www.rockdalenewtoncitizen.com/news/school-board-to-name-gym-after-former-coach/article_c1f8c2a1-8cbc-5d4c-8b39-4b235605893e.html.

Starrs, Chris. "Stroud: Local accolades mean the most." *The Citizens,* May 25, 2019, https://www.rockdalenewtoncitizen.com/features/stroud-local-accolades-mean-the-most/article_59dd6e98-7b06-11e9-ad1b-cffd9de9731a.html.

DICKIE V

"When bad things happen in your life, just turn the page and start a new chapter. Don't close the book."
Latoya Jackson

November 8, 1979 – Detroit, Michigan: NBA Detroit Pistons owner Bill Davidson drove to coach Dick Vitale's house and, without beating around the bush, began with, "Dick, we're making a coaching change. You're fired." It was the low point in forty-year-old Vitale's life. He had never failed in a coaching job. He felt like his life and career were over.

Dick Vitale grew up in a large, blue-collar, Italian family in Garfield, New Jersey. He became a sports fanatic from listening to his eight uncles debate the greatest sports heroes at family gatherings. He loved any sport that involved a ball.

Growing up, Vitale played all sports despite having lost sight in his left eye from an accident at age four. Because his left eye drifted, he was often bullied. When Vitale pitched in Little League, opposing players shouted, "Watch out! Ole one-eye can't see where he's throwing the ball." His mother routinely consoled him, "Richie, don't listen to them. God made you special. You have too much passion for anyone to ever hold you back." Vitale dreamed of being a basketball star but there was just one problem: he wasn't very good.

His first job was teaching sixth grade and coaching basketball at his high school alma mater in Garfield, New Jersey. After seven seasons and two state championships, he became an assistant basketball coach at Rutgers University in 1971. To the surprise of some, two years later Vitale became the head basketball coach at Detroit University. At thirty-four, he was the youngest basketball coach in the country.

After two NCAA tournament appearances, Vitale's meteoric rise in the coaching ranks continued. He became coach of the NBA Detroit Pistons. His first team won thirty games but lost fifty-two. Vitale was not accustomed to losing and didn't handle it well. During the season, he was hospitalized for a week with stomach ulcers. Twelve games into his second season, Davidson showed up at Vitale's house.

After losing his job, Vitale sat on the sofa watching soap operas, whining to his wife, Lorraine, and pondering his future. A month later, he got a call from TV sports producer Scotty Connal who was starting a new network called ESPN. Connal wanted the coach to be an announcer. Vitale burst out with, "ESPN? It sounds like a disease. What is ESPN?" Connal explained his plans for the all-sports channel and Vitale reacted, "Absolutely no way. I know nothing about TV. I want to get back to where I belong, college coaching." He hung up.

With Lorraine's encouragement, Vitale reluctantly called Connal back and accepted a position with the fledgling sports channel until a college coaching position came open. On December 5, 1979, Vitale was on TV as the color commentator for the first college basketball game ESPN aired between DePaul University and the University of Wisconsin. He had a lot to learn, but his colorful coverage of players and his passion for the game won fans over. After the season, with no coaching openings of interest to him, Vitale agreed to stay on for another season.

In 2008, three decades after Dick Vitale, fondly known as "Dickie V," accepted a temporary job at ESPN, he was inducted into the Naismith Basketball Hall of Fame. In 2019, he was honored with the Lifetime Achievement Award for Sports at the 40th annual Emmy Awards—the highest honor in broadcasting.

In August 2021, Vitale underwent multiple surgeries to remove a melanoma. Three months later, he was diagnosed with lymphoma, then a few weeks later with pre-cancerous dysplasia on his vocal cords. He missed his first ESPN basketball season in more than forty years. On April 14, 2022, after a successful vocal cord surgery and six months of chemo to treat his lymphoma, 82-year-old Dick Vitale rung the cancer-free bell.

"Getting fired at Detroit was the best thing to ever happen to me," Vitale said. "Bill Davidson opened the door for me at ESPN. Look at me, I have one eye, I'm not the best-looking guy and I make a great living announcing a game I love. It has been awesome, baby!" Vitale plans to return to ESPN in the fall of 2022 for his 43rd season.

REFERENCES

Dunnavant, Keith. "Season 1, Episode 6: Dick Vitale." *American Achiever,* Podcast, February 7, 2022, Website, 56:22. https://www.americanachievers.us/episodes/episode-6-dick-vitale.

Knight, Joey. "To Honor Dick Vitale's 80th Birthday, here's eight things to know about 'Dickie V' Indefatigable college hoops ambassador and Tampa Bay sports fan Dick Vital turns 80 on Sunday." *Tampa Bay Times,* June 7, 2019.

Moran, Malcolm. "Dick Vitale: Frustrated But Still." *New York Times,* February 1, 1979.

Vitale, Dick. "Hall Call is Simply Awesome." ESPN, September 3, 2008. https://www.espn.com/espn/dickvitale/news/story?id=3566939.

"Dick Vitale." Wikipedia, Wikipedia Foundation. June 7, 2022.

PROPELLED BY LOVE

"Love never gives up, is always hopeful, and endures through every circumstance."
1 Corinthians 13:7

January 7, 2015 - Deerfield Beach, Florida: Robert Konrad left the marina in his 36-foot Grady White fishing boat. It was a beautiful South Florida day, and he planned to do some fishing. Konrad headed the boat east into the Atlantic Ocean, set the autopilot at five miles per hour, and starting trolling. At 12:30 p.m., while he was fighting a fish, a big wave hit the boat knocking Konrad overboard.

He watched helplessly as the boat continued eastward. He had grown up around boats on the north shore of Boston and was keenly aware of his predicament.

Konrad, who was alone and not wearing a life jacket, knew from having recently checked the boat's GPS that he was roughly nine miles offshore. The water temperature was in the low 70s. He also knew that typical survival time at that temperature was three to four hours and that it was not likely he was going to survive. He had two options: wait to be rescued or start swimming. Thinking of his two daughters, he decided to try to save himself, so he stripped down to his underwear and started swimming west toward the shore.

Konrad played high school football at the prestigious St. John's Preparatory School in Danvers, Massachusetts, and was selected to the *Parade Magazine* All-America Team his senior year. He had a great college football career as a linebacker and fullback at Syracuse University and earned a degree in finance and business. Konrad was the last player at Syracuse to wear No. 44, which had previously been worn by college football legends Jim Brown, Ernie Davis, and Floyd Little.

Selected by the Miami Dolphins in the second round of the 1999 National Football League draft, Konrad played fullback for the Dolphins for six seasons until retiring in 2004. While playing with the Dolphins, he obtained his financial advisor certification and started a company to assist NFL players in managing their investments. By 2015, Konrad was living in Deerfield Beach, married, the father of two daughters, a very successful CEO of Alterna Financial, and one of the Managing Directors of KT Capital Partners.

After taking his life into his own hands in the cool water of the Atlantic, Konrad began to swim, alternating between the breaststroke and backstroke. He figured it would take him ten hours, if he made it, to reach the shore. He had never been a strong swimmer but blocking for Miami Dolphin quarterback Dan Marino for six years had taught him toughness, determination, and learning how to push past pain. Although he was swimming across a four mile per hour current that was pushing him slowly north parallel to the shore, by early evening Konrad began to think that maybe he could survive.

Just before dark, a recreational boat passed within fifty yards of Konrad, but he was unable to get their attention. He swam on—more convinced that he would have to get himself to shore. Prior to sunset, Konrad used the sun to keep him swimming in a westerly direction and after dark an occasional glimpse of light on shore served as his beacon of hope.

When he had failed to return by dinner his wife had alerted the Coast Guard, and they began searching for him. About midnight, a Coast Guard helicopter flew directly over him and had him in their lights but did not see him. The minutes that followed were especially difficult. Exhausted, cold, and not sure how close he was to shore, it was his love for his two young girls, ages ten and eight, that inspired him to keep swimming.

At 4:30 a.m., after sixteen hours in the water, Konrad knew he could not hold on much longer when he heard a noise. Confused, and a little disoriented from cold and fatigue, he realized he was hearing waves breaking on the beach. Shaking uncontrollably, and unable to walk, Konrad drug himself up on the sand and collapsed into a ball to try to warm up. He eventually staggered to a Palm Beach oceanfront home where a security guard happened to be making his rounds. Konrad was taken by ambulance to a local hospital where he was treated for hypothermia and dehydration.

Coast Guard authorities estimated that he swam an unbelievable twenty-seven miles to make it to Palm Beach. At a press conference two days later, 38-year-old Konrad told the media, “It was a boater’s nightmare. I am happy to be here—I shouldn’t be here. I’ve got two beautiful daughters; I was going to hit shore.” His wife, Tammy, added, “It was a miracle he made it home. Rob never quits. He swam with two angels on his back.”

REFERENCES

Harding, David. “Former Miami Dolphin Fullback Robert Konrad Swims 9 Miles to Safety After Falling from Boat off Florida Coast.” *NY Daily News*, January 9, 2015.

James, Michael S. “Investigation Closed on Ex-Miami Dolphin’s Boating Accident, 16-Hour Swim.” *ABC News*, February 25, 2015.

Leitch, Will. “Robert Konrad.” *Wealth Management Magazine*, February 1, 2005.

Walters, John. “An Unforgettable Story of Survival…or Just an Unbelievable Story.” *Newsweek*, January 9, 2015.

NOBODY EVER SAW A BALL PLAYER LIKE THIS ONE

"If we make the most of what we have been given, and find our own way of doing things, you wouldn't believe what can happen."
Jim Abbott

September 4, 1993 – Yankee Stadium – Bronx, New York City: He stood on the mound in the eighth inning at Yankee Stadium. For a long moment he studied the scoreboard in center field and thought back on his life. He was just six outs away from pitching a no-hitter—a dream he had imagined since childhood. He was the most improbable of boyhood heroes.

He reflected, "I am here because my dad wouldn't let me whine or quit on the playground as a kid. I am here because my Little League coach and my high school coach believed in me when there wasn't much to believe in. I am here because this thing was not going to defeat me." Jim Abbott got his no-hitter that day, beating the Cleveland Indians 4-0. It was one of the highlights of his major league career.

Mike and Kathy Abbott were shocked when, in Flint, Michigan in 1967, their baby was born without his right hand. They told young Jim that he did not have a disability, but a gift and that he was special for being born that way. Refusing to be a shield for their son, Mike put a baseball in Jim's left hand shortly after he started walking.

When Jim was eight years old, he drew a strike zone on the brick wall on the side of his house and threw a rubber-covered baseball against the house for countless hours. He imagined himself a big-league pitcher, and it was here that he mastered fielding with one hand.

When preparing to pitch, he put his glove on the end of his right forearm. After releasing the ball, he would quickly slip his left hand into his glove to field the ball bouncing off the house. Through the years, at every level of baseball, teams would try to take advantage of his disability by repeatedly bunting against him. They were never successful.

In 1989, after a stellar college baseball career as a left-handed pitcher at the University of Michigan, Abbott was drafted number eight overall in the first round of the Major League Baseball draft by the California Angels. The scouting report read: "6' 3", 180 pounds, great arm, natural cutter fastball, good athlete, good hitter, big competitor…has no right hand." Abbott went directly from the University of Michigan to the California Angels without ever playing in the minor league. He pitched for five teams in his 10-year major league career spanning from 1989 to 1999. His career record was 87 wins and 108 losses.

"I wasn't a great major league pitcher," Abbott says, "but I experienced great moments like the no-hitter with the Yankees. I made it to each level of baseball because of the people who did not give me a chance and the many more who did. Throughout my life, I wanted to be a baseball player, not a one-handed baseball player, so I had to work harder."

Disabled children came to see Jim Abbott in every major league ballpark he played in. Parents brought them—kids who were missing hands, arms, legs, or those who were blind. They brought their children hoping Jim's story would inspire them and help them understand that the spirit inside them was greater than their disability. Abbott always signed autographs until the last kid left. He answered every letter that kids sent to him stating, "I knew how far a kid could run on fifty words of assurance."

REFERENCES

Abbott, Jim and Brown, Tim. *Imperfect—An Improbable Life.* New York City: Ballantine Books, 2012.

Foss, Mike. "20 Years Ago Today, a one-handed Yankee Pitched a No-Hitter." *USA Today,* September 4, 2013.

"Jim Abbott: Motivation Speaker, Professional Baseball Player." Accessed November 2, 2020, www.jimabbott.net.

"Jim Abbott." Players, *Baseball Reference,* Accessed November 2, 2020, https://www.baseball-reference.com/players/a/abbotji01.

www.ingramcontent.com/pod-product-compliance
Lightning Source LLC
LaVergne TN
LVHW020705110826
845149LV00012B/2106